Hoodoo For Beginners

The Ancient Power of Divination, Rituals, Magic Spells, Conjure and Rootwork At Your Fingertips

Jessica Mostafa

Table Of Contents

Introduction

I want to begin this book by asking you some questions: Do you ever feel down on your luck or like things just aren't going right for you? Are you having trouble landing a decent job, or are you tired and stressed all the time?

Have you felt a presence in your home, such as an invisible pressure on your shoulders or back? Have you ever felt like you are forever breaking things or losing items?

Would you believe me if I said that this might actually be because of bad energy in your home and in your life? Would you believe me if I told you that you have the power to control these energies while you may not realize it?

Would you believe me if I told you that something thousands of years old that is rooted in magic, prayer, and faith could help?

This method, or faith, is called Hoodoo.

Hoodoo is a spiritual and religious energy with roots in Africa, the American continent, and even European culture. It is a faith built on ancestry and hope for a better future, forged in hiding.

Although Hoodoo is sometimes shown in films and books like it is this big, bad, evil thing, in truth, it is something much different from that. It is something that may defy your expectations, opening your eyes to a much brighter world.

I know what you think that there cannot be any truth to this, but you'll be surprised to find that magic is, in fact, everywhere. People have accurately predicted disasters, cured illness, and removed spirits from cursed places.

Hoodoo comes from our African heritage and is influenced by and has grown within many other cultures. Hoodoo's teachings come from the experiences of those displaced in the slave trade, who had to hide their practices from their masters.

It is interesting, therefore, that there are a lot of parts of Hoodoo that focus on cleansing evil spirits, bringing good fortune, and removing negative energies from home.

And that is where our time together comes in. When you reach the end of this book, you will have completed a journey of knowledge and discovery. You will be able to cleanse, spiritually heal, and pray to the spirits to bring the goodness of life to you.

We'll cover some basic spells, mojo bags, and even how to cleanse your house of bad energy. I'll also fill you in on some of the essential items you'll need to have in place.

We'll get into what things influence Hoodoo and what music means to the culture—how this music informs rock and roll and the influences of African music on classic art. I hope that by the end of our journey, you are more than capable of taking the next step and getting into the deeper parts of the culture.

We'll look at our roots, ancestors, blood, and the Bible. We will also look at the reasons for using natural ingredients when we can and how we improvise when we cannot.

We'll cover tips for what to grow, what to buy, how to hex, and how to bless; we'll talk about dreams, and we'll talk about burying items for blessings.

We will cover aspects such as luck, divination, crossroads, zombies, and spirits. Also, we will even touch on some of the darker aspects because learning is as much about understanding as it is about rules.

Throughout the book, we will aim to debunk myths about possession and zombies. We'll look at how to maximize the flow of energy in the home. We will even go over magic that heals, or that makes the user susceptible to better opportunities.

So grab yourself a comfortable chair and notebook because this is both a journey and a series of lessons. By the time you finish, you'll be just that little bit more enlightened to create a map of where to go next (and maybe even a recipe book for your spells).

CHAPTER I

What Is Hoodoo?

What is Hoodoo? This is the first question that is always asked. Thus, it is where we will exactly start our journey. It will also be where our journey ends because understanding everything about Hoodoo is a lifetime of spiritual discovery.

While this really is a question that will require some heavy work to even partially answer, it is an interesting question to ask all the same.

You can ask a hundred people this question, and you'll almost certainly get different answers. This is because of misconceptions or assumptions about the belief system, both from the aspect of what it is to what it entails, along with the question of whether it is benevolent or malevolent.

In my personal experience, as well as in the experiences of others, whenever you talk with someone about Hoodoo, especially someone who does not truly know about the subject, they start talking about demons or witches, or even raising the dead. This is because they don't actually know what Hoodoo actually is.

4

This is the first thing we need to talk about at some length because there is an idea that Hoodoo is bad. Some believe that it is all about curses, or hexes, as they are termed. And while these do exist, they aren't the only aspects of this religion.

When slaves were taken from Africa, a lot of the culture was displaced as well. Thus, Voodoo and other religions were mixed with the white Christian and Catholic cultures of the slave masters of the time. This led to the acts of magic by saints in the Bible to be seen as a sign that God and the spirits were in support of slaves.

Jesus himself turned water to wine and healed the blind. Hoodoo also draws some inspiration from Wicca, as spells can be cast using Hoodoo methods. When we cast a spell in Hoodoo, we call it laying tricks or throwing tricks.

There are also a lot of areas that share ideas with Native American beliefs. This is likely to do with the fact that both of those peoples were forced into oppression by the slave culture.

However, as I mentioned at the beginning of this chapter, there is a common idea asserting that Hoodoo and those who practice it are evil.

Hoodoo is not about good, and it is not about evil; instead, it is about creating a balance in life, it is about acceptance of life, and it's about the soul. It is *not* about skin color or where you are from, but instead, it is about a deep-rooted respect for what was, what is, and what will be.

Hollywood Hoodoo

We have all seen those films where there's a scared teen in some lost part of Africa or deep in South America hiding in a cabin filled with animal debris as a maniacal priest with a gold tooth rants about wanting to cut her heart out for the sun god. Or perhaps in the film you've seen, there is a maniacal scientist using ritual sacrifice to resurrect the dead and use them as slaves in his warfare against the heroes.

While gold teeth are a sign of wealth in some places, I am afraid this is the only part of these movies that carry any truth.

Hoodoo on the big screen, little screen, or even in books is usually defined as this all-powerful evil influence where the users make blood and human sacrifices to punish the good. But the truth is this is a Hollywood lie—a story told to scare people with things they don't understand.

Like in the example of our maniacal scientist, did you know the modern-day zombie has its roots in Africa? It originates from Hoodoo and Voodoo's beliefs that they could bring the living back from the dead. In fact, one of the earliest zombie films, *White Zombie*, references this kind of magic.

I make this point because cinema has moved from blaming culture and magic to blaming science for zombies' appearance—just an interesting little fact.

Also, more interestingly, the idea of zombies and their resurrection stems from the African fear of eternal slavery. This fear of being reborn and trapped in a decayed body for eternity in enslavement is where modern zombies come from, and it had little to do with eating brains.

We often are told in books like Dean Koontz's *Darkfall*, where the villainous priest is the antagonist, that magic is only used for nefarious means, and users must be stopped before unleashing a supernatural evil upon the world.

However, all of these tales come from fear and misunderstanding.

Hoodoo is not used for conjuring the devil, nor would it be. But in Hollywood, time and again, you will see the African priest conjuring a demon or monster.

Interestingly, as time goes on, more and more people open up to the possibilities of the spiritual and the magical. I think this is because religions aren't as powerful as they were during the eras past.

Talking about magic is more acceptable in the world now. And this is a good development not just for Hoodoo, but for the human soul.

Voodoo to Hoodoo

One question I find myself getting asked almost without fail is this: How are Voodoo and Hoodoo different? While there is a little bit of an interpretation here, I'll best summarize, and it is a deeply complex and subtle nuance.

Voodoo is the origin—the beginning. It is part of the faith that comes from Mother Africa. Hoodoo is what was born in America; it is the parts that mixed with Christian and Catholic beliefs that blended some of the Native American beliefs.

We draw lessons of the spiritual and the divine from those around us and add the ancestral flavor of Africa, and this is where Hoodoo is formed.

Through our understanding of this, we begin to see the importance of symbolism and evolution in Hoodoo, meaning the ability to adjust, adapt, and grow. This comes from the fact that slaves were afraid to practice in public spaces for fear of being tried and hung for witchcraft.

Witchcraft and the persecution of witches reflects strongly in Hoodoo, as both were seen as an evil, devil-worshipping practice. The truth instead was that the practicing witches were trying to cure or bless, much as we do in Hoodoo.

Conjure

Also known as tricks, and sometimes, instead of Hoodoo, the word conjure is used to describe the magic itself—the prayers, blessings, and cleansings. This is because you are conjuring or communicating with your spirits.

This is something you are always doing, be it in prayer when you are asking a spirit for guidance or while asking a spirit to bless the food you cook.

Even traditional dishes like gumbo are prepared in a way to show thanks to the ancestors and spirits, making this part of the traditions of Hoodoo and conjure.

Many people interchange the words Hoodoo and conjure. In fact, even when you speak of someone who practices Hoodoo, you may simply call them a Hoodoo man. There are proper terms we can use, and we will come to those.

Again, there is a fair amount of misconception as the mainstream media tends to lump it all in under the umbrella of "black magic," which is a misnomer considering the spiritualism at the core. But for now, rather than get into that, I think we need to look at another side of Hoodoo.

God and Conjure

Whenever we followers of Hoodoo say "God," we mean Yahweh, the Christian God. God is important to Hoodoo, but not essential; we can acknowledge God without worshipping Him, although this is something that not all believers of Hoodoo agreed on.

If you believe in other deities, and that is an important part of your faith, you'll need to learn to acknowledge God, but Hoodoo is about the blend.

If you read the Bible with the understanding that God is a powerful spirit and that He acts through magic, you will begin to see the truth that God and magic go hand in hand.

Interestingly, the Bible is used in many practices, from prayer to its utilization as a talisman during chanting. This is because of the protective energies of God.

Folktales

Many African folktales, as well as tales of Africans displaced by the slave trade, inform how, where, and why we pray. Even things like dancing counterclockwise or the kinds of water we use are all drawn from these shared experiences.

However, there are people we know existed who form the basis of the beliefs and misconceptions of Hoodoo.

In 1834, a white couple named Madam and Doctor La-Laurie fled New Orleans. They had lived in their beautiful home until a fire burned it, damaging some of the house. Firemen then found the corpses of slaves in the attic of the home.

It was reported that these slaves had been experimented on, their bodies broken and butchered. It was also later discovered that more remains were buried under the floorboards.

To this day, that house, now a popular tourist site, is haunted. Many believe that it was magic that caused the blaze to end the suffering of the slaves.

These folktales warn of the tricks that mischievous spirits will play on the unwise or of the shortcomings of their heroes. A great many of these stories are told with joyous humor and with a knowledge of how challenging life can be.

It is interesting, therefore, that many wanted for centuries to portray African denizens as uneducated savages.

Laveau

One of, if not the, most famous names in Voodoo or Hoodoo, Marie Laveau was a queen of magic who was born sometime in the late 1700s or early 1800s. She was born a mulatto, which is a local word for mixed race, specifically Spanish or French and black. This means that she was a person of color born free.

Her faith included concepts from both Catholicism and Voodoo, and interestingly, she was known to have conducted Voodoo magic in the Catholic cathedral. Marie was very much against slavery and public executions.

Stories about her power are a rich part of our heritage. One such story claims that a rich man approached her to help his son, who was either accused of rape or murder (though there are a few versions of this story). Marie prayed for days on end for the man's son. She also snuck some tricks into the courthouse, which she put under or near the judge's chair. Sure enough, the young man was found not guilty.

Now, this story falls very much into folktale as there are many detractors of it who suggest that Marie actually had some political influence. However, there is one story that cannot be denied.

Two men were scheduled for execution on July 17th, 1850. Leading up to this event, Marie visited both of them in their cells, praying and blessing them. As stated earlier, Marie was very much against this kind of capital punishment, as it was something of a spectacle.

The day of execution came, and the two condemned men were on the gallows, nooses around their necks. As the men were read their rights, the sky turned black, and thunder, lightning, and torrential rain appeared, as if from nowhere.

Undeterred, the executioner pulled the lever of the trap door, and the two men fell all the way to the floor, falling out of their nooses. With the people stunned, the execution was postponed. There had been hundreds of witnesses, including Marie Laveau.

The result of this seemingly botched execution was such that public executions were banned, but those in attendance knew that powerful magic had been involved.

Although Marie died in 1881, her importance to all of the African cultures cannot be denied. And whilst some of the stories of her power and influence are contested, her influence over the community cannot be.

Even so long after her passing, she is said to haunt New Orleans and that practitioners can pray to her spirit for help and guidance. In her own way, she has become one of the very deities she once prayed to.

Culture

No one culture claims to be the home of Hoodoo. In fact, it is a blend of many cultures—Native American and European as well as Creole, Yoruba, Treme, and others. This melting pot brings colors, sounds, flavors, and ideas from many parts of the world.

Some of the words we use are defined by these blended cultures. For example, where a Hoodoo witch or priest may be a Bokor or Caplata, they can also be Hoodoo man or woman; Haitian influences may lead us to refer to them as Houngan or Mambo.

This interchangeable language is a reflection of the multitude of influences and tribes that fed into the lineage over centuries. So, for the most part, people will have knowledge of a few ways of saying the same thing.

You can even see this in how we refer to Africa. Many followers of Hoodoo will simply use different words or reference separate parts of Africa, such as saying Guinea but meaning Africa.

This idea of using various terms for different aspects is built from the melting pot of languages that our ancestors were exposed to hundreds of years ago. English, French, Portuguese, and many African dialects are all part of the makeup of those chapters of Hoodoo's heritage.

CHAPTER II

Practices of Conjure

When we talk in general terms about Hoodoo, there are many interchangeable words that we regularly use, including the word conjure.

Conjure borrows from many parts of African heritage to form its practices, from the items used to how they are used. Here I'll share with you some of the materials we can use, some of the traditional items, and the kind of conjure magic you can perform.

Later in our journey, I will show you how to perform certain spells, but here we are just talking about the very basic ideas.

I want to point out that some of these ideas, especially when considering improvisation, could feel a little weird at first, and that is normal; those feelings pass with time. You'll feel that way because your mind is trained to be skeptical, and this is okay.

The moment will come when those skeptical feelings will move away, and you'll feel the empowerment of the spirits.

First, we will take a look at the kinds of items you can use, and then we will dive into what we generally want to gain, how it benefits us, and how these benefits can be apparent in everyday life.

What We Use

While we will come to learn that a great many adjustments can be made, there is an importance to what we use in conjure. This is because these things all have different properties. Consulting a Hoodoo man may be a good place to start.

That said, there are many herbs and spices we use in cooking to bring in that flavor of Africa. Berbere, za'atar, saffron, and cumin are all common spices used in cooking. Keep in mind, though, that these can also form part of conjure for use in tricks, mojo bags, or blessings.

The smells of these spices transport us to our ancestral home. However, these are just part of the rich tapestry of what we are trying to accomplish.

Oils are another important part of conjure. Avocado oil, baobab, moringa, and passionflower are all just some of the oils we use. These can be utilized in beauty products, cleaning supplies, and self-cleaning.

Again, like the spices, oils can be used in a variety of ways, and what you may notice is you are drawn to specific oils and spices. This is the will of the spirits, guiding you to the materials you need.

When we blend some oils together, we can make seals or
tonics. These two things can be used in a variety of ways,
from powering up spells to sealing bags or medallions.

We use soil in various ways, as well, because Mother Earth
is powerful and protects us. We also use metals, stones,
and crystals.

Medallions, pendants, or anything else that carries a personal value can grow to be deeply powerful when used in
Conjure. These can be saint figurines, crosses, coins from
ancestors, or bone carvings, which are especially powerful.

Candles are important to us because they allow us to bring
the element of fire into our prayer, as soil brings earth to
our prayer, and air is all around us. Water is powerful too;
bathing rituals will make up part of our rituals.

We will cover many of these things in a little more detail
as we go, but I thought we'd touch on what we use here,
because there are a lot of little things that need to be considered.

Why We Work

There is a large importance in doing the work, and a great
many ancestors would agree with this. I know that you
may be asking yourself, why don't I just buy a premade
spell or have someone do the work for me? Well, in truth,
you can. There are definite benefits to doing the work
yourself, however.

But there are also benefits to seeking a more experienced
practitioner. The main ones involve the guidance you
receive, the lessons you learn, and the different perspec-
tives you gain. With that said, in doing the work ourselves,

we show that we are committed and invite those positive spirits into our lives.

Yes, we should build a network of more experienced people who can guide us or give us tips regarding how to fix a spell that isn't working or that is proving to be tricky.

With time and experience, of course, you might get to the stage where others come to you for advice and for guidance, at which point you can pass on any or all of the knowledge you have accrued.

I suppose this is another reason why we work: we are then able to help keep the traditions of our people alive and well.

What We Can Gain

A consistent question you get asked when you are practicing is this: What do you get out of it? People expect to get fluffy, overhyped answers as if magic and its practice is foolproof.

The truth is complex, though, because it really does depend on what you ask for and how you request it. What preparations we made, our mood, the energy of our homes, and many similar factors play a role in the end result.

When we conjure a spirit for its blessing, we gain its energy, and we gain its wisdom. It will guide or advise us, helping us to see more clearly the right path, or it will lead us to the right place.

Spirits will allow us to see the answer to tough choices and enable us to endure hard times that come our way. They can only take us so far; however, we must build up trust in a way that our relationship is beneficial for each party involved.

As we build this relationship with spirits through prayer and ritual practices, we will come to learn that they can guide us through silence when we are not asking the right questions.

As we come to know this, we can better understand what our ancestors want for us, as well as how to ask the right questions in the right way.

We can influence things like luck, relationships, and money through spells, although these spells don't always work in the literal sense. For example, you may pray for help financially, and the spirits might lead you to an opportunity.

Then, it is up to you to be receptive to this opportunity. You cannot always see with tired eyes, and you cannot always hear when you do not want to listen.

Old and New

Where some ideas evolve over time, becoming entirely unrecognizable from their origins, some are able to keep their older elements whilst adapting. This is very much the case with Hoodoo as it is a blend of old and new.

Hoodoo is a spiritual religion of accepted change. It takes the forced changes of the old world, this is true, but it turns these into something that is positive. This adaptation is what makes us strong; it is what makes us ourselves.

Hoodoo does not denounce new ideas like other religions or spiritual beliefs. It does not claim that a new idea is somehow wrong or not welcome. Part of this is because of the many African tribes—their tribal deities and dialects—that fed into the pot of our ancestors.

When something new is added to this mix, it is not met with fear but with interest. This is one of the main advantages of Hoodoo over other belief systems. We are not afraid of the physical world. Instead, we talk to spirits and draw their energy from the world.

This blend of old and new can be seen in modern solutions for old problems. An example is when we look to other sources for herbs to do the job we need or to new oil blends to fix a boss.

Fixing a boss means being able to make a plantation owner leave you and your family be and to make sure they do not fire the husband.

Now, while plantations no longer exist, fixing a boss or a job is still important, so the old magic adapts to the new world. Having access to materials traditional to Africa is not essential in our practices. However, in the modern world, it is actually more viable than ever.

The invention of the internet has revolutionized the world. You have the option of easily ordering traditional herbs from the comfort of your home.

Music

Music is a big part of our beliefs and helps inform our energy. Vibrations and frequencies from music charge our bodies and our souls with power. I would always advise looking into purchasing some traditional items, wooden rattles, etc. However, I also know that it is possible to get these vibrations in other ways.

Buying CDs or cassettes of tribal music is a good way to substitute buying instruments, but you can also create a drum. Again, improvisation is key. Below we will go through the steps for making your own drum.

What you need: Either a small bucket or garbage pail, cloth sheet, herbs and oils, and string.

1. For this, start with the cloth sheet. It needs to be big enough to cover the bucket's open end. Soak the sheet and string in a blend of herbs and oils. You can determine what is utilized based on either the spell you intend to use the drum for or things that empower the individual playing.

2. Once the sheet and string are soaked, take it out and hang it to dry. If it is summer, outside drying is preferred. Then, pull the sheet over the open end of the tub.

3. The string can then be wound around the tub. Tying the sheet in place, be sure to keep the sheet tight. Once you tie off the string and everything is pulled tight, cut off the excess.

4. This is now a makeshift drum of your own creation. It shows that you are serious and that you want the spirits to see your intent. Painting the tub or adding symbols of power or for the spirits themselves is also a good practice.

Another instrument you can make is a basic rattle:

You will need: small pebbles, rice, an old coffee tin with its lid, and paint.

1. Clean the coffee tin out with Florida water, then let it dry. You'll then want to paint the tin and outside of the lid. You can add the symbols of the different spirits that can protect you. Legba is a good example, as he is the guardian of the crossroads, so can allow you access to sacred places.

2. Once painted and dried, put in a handful of uncooked rice, preferably white, add in the pebbles (smooth and round if possible). You then re-secure the lid with glue, but at first try without out as you may want to add more stones or rice to find a sound that feels right to you.

You now have a rattle and a drum. You could take the time to make extra instruments, as well. A big part of the culture is taking what you have and making it work.

Hexes

Magic comes in many forms—good, bad, neutral—but all magic comes at a price. This can be the cost of items needed for a spell, an offering made, or the soul of the caster.

Hexes are bad spells, tricks, curses, or whatever other words you want to use. These are spells with bad intent. All magic has a mirror, and good and bad exist; this is something that many spiritual belief systems do not assert.

Hoodoo is balance; it is the understanding that we are all capable of good and evil. It is trusting in the spirits to show us that the things we are doing are for the right reasons or with the right magic.

But this magic is still important, as is understanding the consequences that can come for those who play with the dark side of Hoodoo. Blessing someone's house is not going to get you in trouble with the spirits, but putting a hex on their home might.

Asking for someone to have bad luck or to have sickness has a price, but this price can be paid in offerings, normally crops or produce.

The toll these spells take spiritually may not be worth the act of using them, especially if the target is protected.

Boo Hag

When we die, our spirits can return to God, but they can also choose to stay on Earth as part of the spirit world.

If you do good, you're a good spirit, but spirits that are bad and that create hexes and cause trouble are considered "Boo Hag."

If you begin hexing people all the time, the Boo Hag may come and visit you and bring you bad luck or put bad energy into your home. You'll know this is happening because you'll feel it in your bones.

Crossroads

Crossroads are powerful for many reasons in the culture, but for now, I wanted to talk about a tradition that you can implement in some form right now.

If you eat sardines, you are likely to have small metal tins left over. If so, give these a nice rinse, and put a small photograph of an ancestor or loved one into them. Add to this either some roots or stones (both, if you feel the magic calls for it).

Find a crossroad. Now, this is where I must explain that Legba is a spirit with great power who is a crossroad guardian. As we go further into the power of Hoodoo, we'll talk about him a lot. However, here, let's just say burying the trinket with a prayer for him is a great blessing.

In some modern stories, demons are summoned this way. While I am sure there is some dark equivalent, ours is little more than an offering. It is a spiritual invitation to your life, you could say.

This works better if you can bury it in the middle of the crossroad, but the edges work well. Obviously, in many cities this will not be possible, but country roads may allow you to do this.

Crossroads are important as they represent spiritual decisions that we make every day of our lives, having to choose our path. We must give to the spirits who are guiding us to the places we need to be to get the most out of our lives.

CHAPTER III

The Foundations Laid Before Us

All buildings have foundations, and all foundations are built into the dirt to give the building the most strength. This is an interesting metaphor, as we need to learn all about the things that give us our strength—our very own foundations.

Hoodoo is derived from Fon and Ewe Vodun; both faiths originate from our ancestors of Africa. These beliefs were hidden from slave masters. It was a combination of Christian, Catholic, and European Witchcraft before growing in America and blending with other cultures on the continent, becoming what is known as Hoodoo today.

This is a phenomenon called "displacement". This particular displacement led to the creation of dozens of religions that feed into Hoodoo, with many tribal ancestors drawing their power from the Earth itself, which is why dirt is so powerful in Hoodoo religion.

But this combination also leads us to see some customs that are closer to spirituality than to traditional religions.

Many followers of Hoodoo embrace that spirituality is a core idea in the belief system. Hoodoo involves not just feeling spirits, but having a relationship with them, praying to them, giving them praise, and holding them in high regard.

We must invite the influence of and ask for favors from the spirits of our ancestors, the Earth, and the elements. This is why we try to incorporate as many elements in our prayers as possible. It is also why we light candles and use water and dirt both in our preparation and our everyday lives.

Many of the acts of practicing in secret and making use of everyday items evolved from the fear of persecution but grew to symbolize the individual's devotion, allowing for the individual to invoke the spirit in their own home, in their own way.

The Ancestors

Who are our ancestors, what do we learn from them, and what do we need to learn from them? There is no society on Earth that did not originate from somewhere else, whether through migration or being forced out.

Every culture and every group on Earth starts somewhere—no exceptions. Some begin through a conquered or discovered land, some evolve through indigenous isolation, and others are changed and born through the hardships of time, tyranny, and oppression.

When the cultures of Africa were displaced and brought to America during the slave trade, many of the African cultures were blended with European cultures, such as Christianity. However, this is not the only influence that guided our ancestors.

Fire and water rituals have some influence from Native American cultures, which at the time of the slave trade were also subject to displacement due to American colonists. It was even then that the culture was fed misinformation.

Christian and Catholic churches saw the African religions as the work of demons or the devil himself. This misinformation around the mystique of the culture came from a place of fear and racial segregation.

Not only did it lead to the attempts to quell these 'savage' beliefs, but it led to our ancestors being afraid of openly practicing. Thus, they began to adjust, evolving the practices to the more private and individual ones we see today.

As African cultures began to blend with Haitian and Caribbean cultures, they started to take on influences of those places, where music began to evolve from the tribal roots to more exciting and dynamic tunes.

Then, after the slaves were freed, in New Orleans, the genre of jazz was born. Music and the vibrations and energy from it is an important part of many African cultures, but this is especially true of Hoodoo.

Over hundreds of years of upheaval, slavery, and oppression, the truth is that Hoodoo was born as a way of protecting fellow slaves and tricking slave masters. It evolved into protecting good people and giving people the power to influence the less-than-favorable sorts around them.

Many Hoodoo practices require praying to the ancestors for guidance and assistance. This is because they are able to see both the past and the possible futures. We also do this to show them that we respect their influence and sacrifices.

Things to Try

We may struggle to grasp some of the concepts with spirits. They may seem like these lofty, impossible feats. In this way, it is good to do physical things to help us build up that conversation.

The easiest of these things would be to either keep a journal or to write letters. Writing letters is probably the easiest, as you need only write what the message is you are looking to say.

You can then bury this letter in your garden. It will be soaked into the soil over time, so it's a really good way of putting messages into this big pool of Mother Earth's energy. Letters are also good for writing out your faith or fears so that you can either share this with Mother Earth or cleanse that fear.

When it comes to journal-writing, the first thing I would do is lightly sprinkle some blessed water on the front cover. If the book is leather-bound this is safe; hardcover notebooks also work just fine.

I'd then address your ancestors each day. This way, you are showing that you are inviting them into your life and home and into your heart and soul.

Gifting trinkets made by hand is another thing, especially if you are blessing these things on your altar, which we will come to do.

You'll know your ancestors are reaching out to you when you begin to feel energy from nowhere, like a tingle or a warm vibration.

Another relatively recent and more well-known thing you could try to do is use an Ouija board, or spirit board. This is a way of communing with spirits, and with the right preparations, could be a good way of communicating with the ancestors.

Deter the Bad Spirits

When we hear the more mainstream assumptions regarding magic, the idea is that it is all the manipulation of dark and cruel spirits. While this is a misinterpretation born of fear and a millennium or more of fear-mongering, there is a hint of fact here.

Some spirits are spiteful or more inclined to curse or hex those who try to make use of magic and power.

Protecting yourself, especially when you are dealing with spirits, is important. However, there are some interesting things you can do, and we will touch on some of these as we go.

But what if I told you that you could use fear to keep a spirit at bay? This is a common way of deterring the spirits unwanted by tribes or individuals, and it is still practiced today. These methods include chants, dances, music, and fire.

Fire is especially effective depending on the spirit, as it can purify. Holy water can also be used to keep these bad spirits at bay, but fire is especially efficient. There are other things you can use, such as salt, baths, or smells. However, there is one item that is especially powerful that may surprise you: the Bible.

Hoodoo and the Bible

It may sound weird at first, but the Bible and Hoodoo share some interesting ties. I know that many of the teachings of the Christian and Catholic faiths show that magic is to be feared, but this doesn't match what we see in the Bible.

We'll talk about the obvious stuff, like Jesus healing the blind and the sick with magic, energy, and prayer. All of these ideals are part of Hoodoo and are what we will most often be looking to conjure—these healings and blessings.

Moses performed hexes, as well, resulting in a horde of locusts. Along with that, his staff became a snake. Moses was powerful with magic, and as such, he is a figure of importance in Hoodoo.

The Bible also teaches us that spirits come in many forms. In John 4:1, we are warned to test the intent of spirits to see if they were sent by God. This may be a reference to angels, but it could also be referring to general spirits.

This is important as it is God acknowledging that spirits can be both good and bad. As such, in Hoodoo we are looking to spirits for guidance constantly, looking for any omens that might mean they are leading us down a bad path.

As part of this integration of faiths, there are those who incorporate hymns and prayers from traditionally Catholic sources into the Hoodoo conjure practices.

History

No matter how important the future is, nothing is more important than our history.

History teaches us many lessons—lessons not just of magic but of our individual truths. And knowing our ancestors is a powerful part of the journey. Researching your family tree and lineage will get you closer to these truths.

Finding out where you came from, what things defined who you are, and how you came to be where you are now is important. This knowledge can lead to learning more traditional herbs and roots to use, things that are ancestrally vital.

One of the most interesting aspects of this is that you could very well learn of a part of your lineage you had no idea about.

This is why I find the availability of genealogy tests intriguing; they can show you where the various parts of your blood come from.

It's always very interesting to see these tests be undertaken, and the subject have a much broader heritage than they realize.

This heritage allows us to understand why we prefer certain smells or tastes. This is our ancestral spirit communicating to us.

One thing I really hope you learn to do is to embrace conversations about the culture you are a part of and your roots. Our identities were denied for a long time, so reclaiming it is going to be a wondrous experience.

As an Influence

Africa has influenced a great many things, but none more than art and music. This allows us to pay homage to Africa in surprising places.

Artists such as Pablo Picasso and Henri Matisse reference African influences in their art, from their sculptures
to their cubist paintings. Ernst Ludwig Kirchner used
the earthen colors and intensity symbolic of Africa in his
work.

African Americans have also influenced music, such as
jazz and rock, via blues music, which itself is an evolution
of tribal music and ululations.

Even today, in pop and country music, we can still hear
the influences of the cultural evolution that blues brought
to music.

Slowly, African folklore is beginning to influence film and
TV in a more positive light, with more traditional stories
being committed to film (such as *His House*). It is telling
that these are being cast in the light of magic rather than
being solely evil.

This is still an issue that needs rebalancing, and as a society, we need to do more to seek equality.

Modern Problems

Times are changing. Racism is still a problem, however.
The Black Lives Matter movement speaks volumes of the
fact that most people want change and balance—that the
idea of vilifying a person or persons due to their color is
unjust.

Hoodoo and African beliefs have had to tackle this issue
more than most, and yet are accepting of others. Many
peoples of various cultures practice Hoodoo and give
praise to the history and power of the culture.

This is because there is an understanding that all people are born of the same Earth, from the same soil, and with the same spirit energies.

We must be accepting of all people—all of God's creations—for if we are not, aren't we denying that God created us all?

This credence of belonging and acceptance is incredibly important to us as a culture, as it removes negativity from us and is a core element of Hoodoo as a spiritual religion.

In the melting pot of modern politics, Hoodoo is growing in popularity, and many black and minority peoples feel as though they need extra protection in an increasingly volatile world.

A Place in the World

There are parts of society that are beginning to shift against the establishment. Made apparent by things such as an increasing number of vegans and bohemians, society has begun to see that the old ways weren't working.

Hoodoo is about the respect of what was, adaptation to what is, and looking forward to what could be, while showing love to oneself and those we interact with.

Our ancestors showed tremendous respect to the earth, and all the things connected to it, and none of those fears of hardships led to hate.

Finding a place in the world is the same as finding peace within the self, and this is an incredibly important lesson for us to learn.

CHAPTER IV

The Power of the Root

There are a great many things in Hoodoo that carry power, this is something you will learn quickly, and magic is not always in things you have to go out of your way to find.

Magic can be found in everyday items and natural materials. Most of these things are all around us in the world, and this is especially true of roots and plants.

When we say rootwork, which is often a term substituting Hoodoo, we mean working with plants, including the literal root, leaves, stems, barbs, pollen, and even the sap of trees.

Roots, much like dirt, are linked with Mother Nature and with the spirit of the world itself, and as such, have incredible power. All roots have some power. While we can't cover them all, we can cover some of the benefits of them.

In this section, we'll talk about some of the most powerful roots. I'll also include some standard plants, and then we can look at their uses and give examples of how to amplify this kind of magic.

This way, the next time you enter an apothecary, you can know what to look for, and you will understand why it benefits you.

I'll also give a few tips concerning how to bring more roots into your everyday life and how, in turn, to empower your home.

As you become more enlightened to the uses and properties of different roots and plants, you'll come to prefer certain ones for certain spells, be it from practical use or ease of access.

Roots and Plants of Note

There are far more plants than I have time to cover, as well as a great many blends of materials that can be used to amplify them. So I found it best to discuss the more prominent and common ones. Unless I note otherwise, these should be somewhat easier to come by than the more exotic items.

First, we will look at tobacco. Unsurprisingly, this is a leaf that is used in many spells and incantations due to its pungent aroma and deep links to Africa. This leaf itself is used in dreaming spells and in drawing in spirits, but it is popular for its availability.

We then have calamus, a medicinal plant. This one can also be used as a spice, which, as I have already mentioned, is a powerful tool in our collection. Calamus appears in some modern medicines, as an extract or as a key ingredient, and it has its origins in Africa.

Also, with any plant like calamus where a treated medicine contains it, I would suggest that you do not try to use the medicine in place of calamus, as the additional ingredients of the medicine may not create the desired spell.

Jezebel root is primarily used for seduction, and the Adam and Eve root pairing is used for love. Both of these take their names from other sources but are readily available through specialists.

Where we have roots known by a specific name or that may have an aphrodisiac quality, replacing them with something with the same effect is advisable. That being said, always keep your eyes peeled for an apothecary as it can help find any specific items.

Licorice (yes, the stuff that is made into candy) is another powerful root, as is lavender, another plant known for its scent and sweet flavor.

Again, I would advise against using candies made from specific materials like this, as they can have artificially produced colors and preservatives. This can lead to issues where the extra ingredients can create unexpected outcomes in the spell or blessing.

Add this collection to one of the lesser-known roots, such as mugwort or angelica, and you'll begin to have a broad range of things you can try.

The easiest thing to do is stick to ingredients you like, but sometimes changing things up is a good idea, so having a well-stocked pantry might be worthwhile.

I would also look into drying out and freezing some items to store them for longer, especially as some materials can only grow at certain times of the year. Making sure you can access tricky materials regularly is a good practice.

Basics of Rootwork

We've covered a handful of useful roots and the potential ingredients that are good to keep an eye open for. We don't, however, know anything about actually doing the work itself.

So, let's look at some more roots and the things you can use to amplify them. This should give you a better idea of how to work with roots in such a way.

High John is a root that can be used to conjure power, money, and masculine sexuality. Let's focus on the power aspect, specifically empowering you as an individual. We'll have a look at things to compliment this root and what you can try.

What you'll need: High John root, mortar and pestle, black salt, oil burner, geranium oil, and a tealight candle. (This is a good time to mention that oil burners and a mortar and pestle are all but essential in our practices.)

1. First, finely cut some High John root and place in the oven on low heat for a few minutes until dried out. Add a pinch of ground black salt, and grind until it is a fine powder. Now you can make more than you'll need, and I recommend that you do, as you'll need more for another spell, no doubt. However, you should also do so just in case you need to try the spell again, whether it is because something went wrong or you get a sign to try again.

2. Put this mixture in the top section of an oil burner, and add the geranium oil. In the lower section, place and light the candle and set this near your bed. The High John brings power, the salt brings protection, and lavender brings healing. This mixture will help you sleep better, keep bad dreams away, and empower you for the day ahead if burned in the morning.

Now that we have one that is for empowerment let's look at some combinations that can be used for money. Here, you'll need a basic money chant. Don't worry, we'll cover chants later, but for now, let's look at what you need.

What you'll need: Onion skin, five finger grass, bay leaves, cinnamon, basil, and dirt.

1. Add a little of each ingredient to your mortar and pestle, grind until crushed, then empty into a small metal tin (empty, cleaned food tins work perfectly) with some dirt from the home.

2. Next, you want to write your debt problems or money concerns on a piece of white paper, rip it into pieces, and add this to the tin, then mix. Next, drop in a lit match, and repeat your chant three times as the mix burns.

3. This can draw money or business into your life or bring you resources to make this happen.

One of the core ideas for using any root is to look at the benefits it is known to have and look for ideas or materials regarding how to best complement this. You may use other roots, herbs, oil, oil blends, or even items such as medallions to raise the potency.

Using items such as onion skin is an indicator of one of the core ideas behind the practices of Hoodoo: we should try to avoid waste as much as possible, so everything should be used.

Do you have cuts of carrots? You can use these in compost to grow herbs and plants, and you can also use them in spells or break them down to stain items with an orange color. Do you have a used chicken carcass? Bones are used in everything from divination to mojo bags, so drying them out and storing them is fine.

Roots at Home

As we have now established, plants carry power that is sacred and influential. This is represented in their smells and energies. As they come from plants, it goes to say that spices and roots carry power as well.

As we want to empower our homes as much as we can, it is time to start growing plants there. Things like mint and lavender can be grown at home. Plants come in many sizes, and each one gives you access to soil (which you'll learn about shortly).

Growing some of your own plants not only gives you access to the plants, but gives you the opportunity to influence the energies in the plant itself. Using blessed water on a plant can purify its power.

There are also practices that show plants respond to positive speech and energies. This gives us the opportunity to practice prayer in an unconventional way, as we can begin to pray to the plant itself.

I would also look into a greenhouse or outdoor storage of some sort, as certain plants need warmer, damper conditions to grow, and, thus, during colder months, they are harder to get hold of.

This greenhouse could also be a place where you can store bags of soil or any items you've collected that you may not want in the house, such as chicken bones.

Hanging protection stones or painting symbols on and in the greenhouse will also keep unwanted spirits from your materials.

By the way, don't panic if you have no plant pots, as jars, jugs, and old plastic tubs work just as well for planting with very alterations. In fact, you could grab a small plastic tub, put some soil in it, and grow mint on any window-sill in your home.

The key here is to make an effort. There is a big difference between "wanting" and "doing" and between "saying" and "doing." And the spirits will see this; someone who truly wants to do something but who is not actually acting may not be in favor of the spirits.

At the Root

In the culture of the modern world, we still use ideas or phrases that come from our pasts. Take the turn of phrase "remove it at the root," for example. Consider just why this phrase is important to us.

When this term is used in the modern world, we are generally talking about removing a group who are committing crimes from society or removing a negative influence from a section of society, like violent movies or games, song lyrics, or images.

The exact origin of the phrase is up for debate, but here's where it applies to us: When a plant has been hexed, for example, a sick crop hexed by a rival farmer, our ancestors would need to remove the affected plant and bless the land.

When the plant is removed, it is not as simple as clipping away the dead part, as the rot or sickness could spread through its roots. This means that they needed to remove the plant at the root.

If a plant has been used for tricks or hexes, it is advisable to remove the full plant at the root if it has come from the home. This ensures that no excess magic is left behind when the plant is disposed of.

This, I believe, is also where the term "the root of the problem" most likely comes from. Of course, the origins of terms is for another book, but it is definitely an interesting consideration.

The Root of All Evil

There is another 'root' statement I think is an interesting one to discuss because I believe it is wrong. It is one of those phrases used to blame something that is an idea, rather than the person committing an act.

"Money is the root of all evil" is a common saying, and while there is an argument here for some form of truth, the fact is people were cruel and evil before money. Many act on cruelty and evil without there being a financial gain.

Not all evil can be attributed to money. And this is important, as it speaks of something you really must understand about the ancestors and the magic we are trying to use.

In Africa, trade was cattle for cattle, crop for crop, milk for an egg, and so on. Money was not the root of the evils that Africans did to each other. Rather, greed, pride, and envy were the roots of evil, and this is still true.

People are capable of wondrous things such as curing disease and creating whole worlds with words. However, people can be spiteful and hateful, and the soul is capable of evil. This is what the world of Hoodoo understands.

Good and evil are both essential. It is a balance; having one without the other is impossible. For example, without the devil, there is no God. And this is where the statement is wrong. Money is not the root of all evil but is simply a modern temptation to feel greed and jealousy.

The truth is, evil originates in the same place as good: in the hearts and souls of regular people who choose their path and walk it, for better or worse.

Recipes

Writing a recipe down and keeping a record of what you used, how much you used, and other steps you took are all very important. The spells you like and that worked should be recorded. This book does not need to be in the home either.

I touched on keeping some items outside of the house in a greenhouse or external storage area, and this can be one of those items.

This book can evolve; any notes you make and any spells you are handed on paper can be stored here. Keeping the book blessed and protected is also important. I would recommend soaking some string in an herb and oils for protection. Then, once dry, you can bind the book in this rope.

This book could then be the focus of your prayer, and as you grow in experience, you'll have a record of all of the things you have achieved. This would be good for you to be able to show the spirits all of the blessings and offerings you have made.

You could also put some photos of ancestors or loved ones in the book to make it a focal point of energy and affection. This then can be used to transfer that energy into the spells and blessings you perform.

However, as I said, you will absolutely want to have a recipe or spell journal. My favorite word for this is a grimoire, which is the common name for a book of spells. Many such books are afforded human names to allow them to be inhabited by powerful spirits.

CHAPTER V

The Power of the Dirt

You will walk on the dirt of the land most every day, a thousand miles and more in a lifetime, but do you ever think of the history and power that you also walk on?

Dirt is the energy of Earth, and Mother Earth is powerful. It is from her that we are all born, and to her, we will all return. It is for this reason that dirt can hold great power, and as such, building sites provide great opportunities, as do gardens.

This is why we take pilgrimages and build our statues and monuments from stone. This is also why people in tribes walk barefoot and why we always have our connection to this dirt in mind.

When we want to bless or lay a hex when we want luck or wealth, or even when we consider our lives, we use the power of dirt; we call on the power of Mother Earth. Some call these ideals bohemian, and perhaps that is the influence (or perhaps Africa is the influence on bohemia).

To bless a house, we must bury an item, which should be something important to us or something dirty and well-used (pillows or sheets are a good example). For instance, you can cut sections off a small strip of a sheet perhaps, tie it in a knot, and bury it in your yard, and then you can use this to bless your house.

If you want your partner to be faithful, you can take some dirty underwear, tie this up in a knot, and bury that in your backyard, and this helps with faithfulness.

Burying items can be a very good way of drawing the right energy and spirits into your life. If you bury an item near a courthouse, it can protect you with the energy of lawfulness, and churches give you spiritual protection.

There are also ways to bless a home with love, good luck, a job, or money. You can also bring bad luck to others.

From padlocks to stones, a great many things can be buried for an array of reasons, and we as a society can but pay tribute to this power. All our crops and all our lives are fueled by the forgiving dirt.

Garden

It is perhaps no accident that one of the most sacred places mentioned in the Bible is a garden. Gardens are an extension of our homes that give us access to our plants and to our dirt.

As we build a garden of flowers or of herbs and spices, or as a lovingly built place of worship, or as a peaceful place of meditation, we channel our gardens with positive energy. In this way, it becomes a sacred place for us. It is where we eat during the warm months and where we party at night.

Our gardens are important, so burying a blessed item charges the area with yet further positive energy. So, when we need dirt for a blessing or a prayer, this is where we can come and know we are getting pure energy.

However, not all dirt is safe to use, and many houses may not have gardens. So what can you do if that is the case? Well, for homes without gardens, like apartments, buying a planter or window box is ideal.

Graveyard Dirt

Graveyard dirt is a powerful thing. It has a lot of emotional and spiritual energy within it, and it is the very structure of ghosts. It is for this reason that I would advise against using graveyard dirt where possible, especially as a beginner.

Graveyard dirt and church dirt can mix at times if the church has a graveyard near it, but using dirt from the side or garden where no one is buried is a good idea.

Again, many spells can call for graveyard dirt, and while many of them are beneficial, as a beginner, I would advise against them in the interim.

What I will say is that this dirt is the most powerful, as it contains the remains of ancestors. Therefore, it is always worth learning a little more about it.

One thing to know about graveyard dirt is that not all people who are buried in a church graveyard are good people. This means this dirt is more likely to contain malevolent energies but is also sure to be more powerful than other dirt.

Using Graveyard dirt in a spell or mojo bag will amplify the magic, but you may see omens warning you to stop. This is because there is magic that is dangerous to mess with if you are inexperienced.

Dirt and Skin in Spells

One thing you will come to learn and will have seen referenced, is that a lot of conjure or tricks involve the use of dirt. This is because dirt carries power within it. Keep in mind that sometimes you'll want to dry the dirt out or add water to it, depending on the kind of spell you are doing.

There are even some cases where adding just a pinch of dirt to a meal during preparation is recorded amongst Hoodoo practitioners. This is to invite Mother Nature and her power into ourselves.

Some spells may call for shavings of skin. This will generally be from the bottom of the foot; pedicure equipment is a good way to get this.

Fingernails and toenails, as well as hair, all can be used in more advanced spells or for very specific hexes. This is because these things are all charged with energy.

Livestock, eggs, flowers—these have all been made as offerings for the deities and are still things that many people do offer. Again, this is because of what they represent.

Giving a piece of hair to our spirits is saying that we want them to share in our power so that we can share in theirs.

Some of these concepts may sound strange or alien, but the fact is that magic comes with a small price—not quite human sacrifices, but a small cutting of a fingernail might suffice.

Paint

I want you to go to any cafe or bar—any store or stockist that is inspired by Africa. You'll see lots of dark brown and red paint, as well as a lot of yellows and whites. Also, these items will be hand-painted and carved.

You may not realize it, but painting is a deeply rooted part of Africa. Part of this is because berries, mud, plants, and even food was used by our ancestors to paint. But partly, this is also because the traditions were focused on making the most out of every item so that nothing was ever wasted.

So many of our preparations may ask us to paint an item. Store-bought paints are fine, but I would always advise that you add just a little pinch of finely crushed dirt to the paint.

Once you have done this you can begin to stir the paint, moving that power through all of it. This, when paired with prayer, can lead to the protection of the house or the item being painted.

One of the things I would definitely recommend that you paint for yourself is your altar. I'd use earthen colors, such as a deep red, for example.

With painting symbols, white is a good color, which is why I said to use dark, earthy colors.

Which leads us to one of the most beautiful items of our ancestry we could look into picking up.

Masks

Masks are a part of our heritage, in much the same way that plants and spices are powerful to us. Masks and the things they symbolize are incredibly important.

Masks were worn during conjure, ritual, dance, for birth, and for death. They are much more than the art they are seen to be now, with their colors being brown, red, white, and black, all drawn from Africa.

Owning one and having it on or near a place where you pray will allow you to focus that energy into the mask itself.

We see masks in a lot of European cultures, such as for balls and masquerades. Also, in England, there was a masked group of doctors who were prevalent during the black plague. These plague doctors live on in modern culture, as they are visually striking.

This is the power of masks—they hide the identity of the wearer, changing them from something very human to something otherworldly. Using this, we can channel that otherworldly energy into the wearer.

Blood

As with graveyard dirt, there are ways to use blood in spells. Many European cultures would use leeches to drain small amounts of blood.

However, blood magic is dangerous because of the power of blood. It is the very energy of life, so using it to manipulate magic will be tricky to get right. However, blood magic is another thing shown in the media as commonplace.

Mostly this is untrue. Again, most spells are done privately and with a level of secrecy, so any blood used is likely from the spell caster. Wearing vials of blood is another exaggeration; while this does happen, it is not very common at all.

I really wanted to touch on blood magic because I felt it would be dishonest not to mention it, and we will get more into it later. Mostly I have heard of animal blood, such as chicken or pig's blood, for example, being used for ceremonies.

But as I mentioned, large scale human bloodletting is a Hollywood myth created to keep an idea of fear of the unknown alive and well. Some people have used human blood in vials to empower their spells. The blood is often their own or menstrual.

And, yes, I know that sounds like a grotesque thing to do, but some people feel they need that level of commitment. I personally do not, and I would advise strongly against it.

Stones and Crystals

There are powers that we may never fully understand, but there are fears and doubts in our souls that can be abated. The modern world is a vast and often confusing place, and as such, more people are turning to spirituality every day.

I have mentioned throughout our journey and will continue to mention that Hoodoo is a spiritual religion. It shares more than a few concepts with the more well-known spiritualism practices, such as reiki, astrology, and numerology.

These common threads are the influences of energy over our everyday lives and how best to amplify the positive energies and remove the negative. There are also examples of spell-casting in some spiritual practices, where a practitioner may be encouraged to meditate while listening to simplistic music.

This form of sound energy is something that is quite common in Hoodoo, where we use drums and rattles to amplify our energies already. But what other modern spiritualism ideas are we likely to use?

Crystals are a great example of a cross-faith item of power. In spiritualism, it is known that these crystals carry power, and in Hoodoo, we know that anything born of Mother Earth carries power.

In this way, we know that crystals and stones generally carry power from Mother Earth within them. In this section, I want to talk about some common stones and crystals and the attributes we can draw from them.

Coral is a good one to start with, as there is a part of our culture informed by Haiti and other Meditteranean places where coral is common. This stone is said to have properties of nurturing and harmony.

These properties could amplify a faithfulness spell or help with a calming charm. With faithfulness spells, in particular, this could be a useful addition to a hex bag if there is a lot of turmoil in the home.

Amethyst is another one that is very common amongst practitioners, as it amplifies spirituality and intuition, and it can aid with cleansing. When we cleanse, we can incorporate amethyst in some way to amplify this.

Amethyst amplifying our spiritualist energies makes it incredibly useful. It could be used as a way of drawing positive energies into the home.

Garnets are very common and get used in a lot of jewelry. This gemstone brings energy, health, and passion. Perhaps best used in a healing or love spell, this stone has a deep plum color that I genuinely adore.

Bloodstone, which draws its name from its red-stained qualities, is said to be stained with the blood of Christ and is therefore incredibly powerful. This stone provides courage and can be used to purify, both incredibly useful attributes.

Other notable stones that I think would come in handy are: Jasper, which amplifies healing, helps you to keep grounded, and calms chaos; Jade, which brings wisdom, peace, and prosperity; and turquoise, which brings luck and healing, but can also help to improve communication.

In this way, we can begin to incorporate the absolute best of the energies in our world and our efforts to commune with spirits.

As for stones, many places of perceived power have standing stones or henges. These places are sites of tremendous energies.

There are also countless examples of the practice of painting stones to act as fairy homes in wooded areas, as well as historical instances of stone being painted with sigils.

The modern equivalent may be a 'Banksy,' an artist who paints political messages in stylized art forms on stone and brick. (This artist has risen to prevalence due to his creative style and elusiveness.)

Stones and the painting of stones is still widely practiced and may have its roots in Africa. That said, it is nice to see any mural, especially if it is one of a cultural kind.

Glass

As I have said, trees are sacred, but bottle trees are an evolution of Hoodoo that is linked solely to its American influences. You see, bottles are used for spells, storage, drinking, and even for holding candles in lieu of a candle-stick.

This flexibility is one part of the value of glass; the other is its source, the earth. All glass comes from superheated dirt or sand, which then crystallizes. This, in turn, allows for the glass to become something new.

Over many hours, it is worked and reworked with fire and dedication to become something stronger. Perhaps there is a parallel with our own culture here, where we have been molded into something else?

In either case, glass items have a reverence that has led to the creation of bottle trees, the practice of putting wishes and protection spells into glass bottles and hanging glass bottles near the house.

This is just another way we can see the evolution of an item (in this example, sand to glass) mirroring the transi-tion of African heritage to the present. This sacredness of glass and its importance to us can be seen in other cul-tures, too.

Most churches have stained glass windows, many cultures believe breaking a mirror is bad luck, and broken glass is commonly used in many dark magics.

CHAPTER VI

How to Perform Cleansing

They say that home is where the heart is, and the heart is an important part of our emotional energy and power. When our heart and soul are not right, everything begins to feel wrong. There are modern words for this wrongness.

We can often feel tired or depressed, and we may not be able to find a reason. Our diet is fine, we exercise, and work isn't too stressful for once. Yet, there is that lingering sensation that something is wrong.

Very likely, there is a spirit in your home or latched onto you that is causing these feelings. This could be for many reasons, which might not always be negative, but when we sense that stress and anxiety, we need to consider the bad spirits.

You see, spirits can actually be both good and bad, and making sure we take time to remove the negative ones can help us.

We are going to perform some cleansing actions, both for ourselves and our home. While some of these seem excessive, they really can benefit you. Cleansing is always a good idea, but it also allows you to start fresh.

When we cleanse spirits, we remove its power over us, and we remove its energy from our homes, selves, and loved ones. Each cleansing is a little bit different, but all of them are about removing that spiteful energy from the thing that is burdened.

As such, one of the most important things for us to do is cleanse the home. This is to remove the negativity, lingering bad spirits, and bad luck, as well as to allow the positive energy to return to the home once more.

It may sound obvious, but you'd be surprised how many homes you'll walk into and feel that bad energy vibrating all around you. This is represented in a modern idea called feng shui, where the room is designed to allow energy to pass through it in a certain way.

Feng shui is the study of energy in the home, and spirits can affect this energy, so perhaps studying feng shui is a good idea. In any event, that is where we start—with some steps on cleansing the home.

Cleansing the Home

It seems obvious, but yes, there is a slight difference between cleaning and cleansing a home. Cleaning is something that should be done regularly. In fact, the difference is similar in concept to the difference between tidying and cleaning.

One is more of a quick fix, while the other is a more involved process of actions you need to undertake. And this is the same with cleansing and cleaning; a clean home is not the same as a cleansed home.

All that being said, let's look at the steps and items for making the home a cleansed place—a spiritual blank slate.

What you will need: buckets, mop, washcloths, Florida water (Zamzam water may be a suitable replacement), empty spray bottle, and soap.

The first thing to know is that you will need to start at the top of the house and at the back of the house. This is important. You will be forcing the old energy out, so open all of your windows.

Mix your Florida water with some plain soap. You will want to start with the back wall in the backroom and clean, scrubbing down all the surfaces and all the ridges in the windows. You will need to scrub every inch.

Move from back to front, then from top to bottom. Once on the lowest floor, move to the back of the house, and once again, clean from the back of the house to the front.

You need to take extra time cleaning outdoor thresholds throughout this process, as spirits can get trapped here.

Once you have cleaned the house, throw the water out of your front door eastwards.

If you have carpet or rugs, you should clean these too. The dirt in them includes mud, dust, and even dead skin. Making sure to wash out all that bad residue is very important at this point. If you have a cloth couch, you're going to want to clean that too.

Wooden furniture is the easiest to clean in this regard, and as we can get those earthen colors in wooden furniture more easily. Thus, I suggest getting a nice wooden table for the dining room.

Removing old furniture, broken pots, or shattered mirrors is also essential. Signs of misfortune draw misfortune to us; As such, making the time to clear these issues from our home is incredibly important.

I would also suggest that removing anything from the house that was used in magic with less than kind intent would be worthwhile. Having aggression and cruelty in the home in any form is toxic and can cause huge issues.

Cleansing the Self

Just like the home, our bodies can become unclean and burdened by the energies of spirits and the world around us. Much like with the idea of cleansing instead of cleaning a house, we all know that bathing and showering instead of a quick wash is better for keeping ourselves clean.

Therefore, it is time for us to have a spiritual bath, and this is actually quite a simple process. You can even buy spiritual bath kits. This will include oils and scents to relax the body and clear the mind.

The water you use should be hot but not scalding. Bath salts are a good idea. In order to get rid of negativity, you need to wash from your crown down towards your toes, but for luck and fortune, you wash from your toes to your crown.

If you have crystals and incense in the room with you, which magnifies those effects, they can be used to bring positivity or wealth into your life.

Using blessed water or Florida water is a good idea, but as this is going to be a lot of water, bath salts are a good substitute.

Surrounding the bath with incense, salts, and candles can also act as a protective barrier for the bath, keeping any unwanted spirits at bay. This is often a good practice when bathing a sick or young person who cannot bathe themselves.

If a person is bed-ridden, making a small bowl of any materials you want to use and having that by the bed so you can lightly wash them is also a really good idea. This will not only cleanse the person but keep them safe and rested.

Cleansing With Fire and Water

There are things that cannot be cleansed in the traditional way we would wash out a food stain or muddy footprint. These things are the lingering aspects of magic, and as such, we need to turn to magic, specifically the elements, to help us.

Elements are an incredibly important aspect of our cultures. Each one is essential in some way.

Fire is one of the essential elements, it is a part of the power of life, and we must respect it at all times, both as an element and as a potentially dangerous power.

Fire is also good for cleansing. We can burn old photos or items that we no longer need. We can write down our fears and our problems and burn those as well.

The act can show the spirits that we no longer need that burden in our lives. We use fire to light our candles and to burn incense. It is one of our elements of power and is present in many Hoodoo beliefs.

In addition to this, we should discuss streams. Running water is often charged with particles of dirt, but also is energy itself. If we wash away used material in water, as long as it is biodegradable, we can use this to carry it away.

This removes the item, but also any excess magic—good or bad—from it. This is also good for gathering water to bless, cleanse, or use for spells, as streams aren't chemically treated. If you are able to find the source of the stream, this water will largely be safe to drink.

Researching your local area for places like this is beneficial, as you'll always have much purer water this way.

These two elements are used as opposites, but function in much the same way, allowing for the removal of unwanted energies and spirits by offering the wanted spirits our devotion and prayers through these energies.

Cleansing With Milk

Some cultures have used milk baths as a symbol of wealth or to make the skin softer and look younger. In fact, in Egyptian folklore, it is said Cleopatra bathed in milk. Bathing in milk is, however, a part of Hoodoo's roots.

This is most especially true in tribes in Africa, where children are blessed with a milk bath; this bath is blessed with herbs and crops local to the tribe.

The more remote tribes are known to have skulls of animals as part of the ceremony. While we won't be covering that, it is an interesting practice to see.

The prayer is normal for health and strength, as the child will likely be enduring the hardships of disease and famine still prevalent in parts of Africa.

Fresh, untreated milk is said to work best. Again, this is likely due to the importance of agriculture and produce to the tribes. The herbs and crops used don't matter as much as their value to the person making the offering.

The spirits know that this gesture matters as it is removing crops from the village; this is more likely to have a positive effect on the spell.

Coconuts

More so because of our ancestors' coastal and tropical influence, coconuts have a special place in our culture. They can be used in spells or as offerings, or they can give us a form of milk that can be used in cleansing or bathing.

They are a source of food that we can utilize in spells and cooking. The fibrous hairs on their shells make for good material for crafting and burning. Also, they can be painted to represent faces and heads, and their shells make for good makeshift bowls.

Having access to coconuts is a really good idea, so stock up on a couple when you see them, and buy coconut milk wherever and whenever possible.

Spring Clean and Detox

Throughout our journey, we begin to see things that society already does that we can begin to do for ourselves. These things include spring cleaning and detoxing, and I wanted to take some time to cover these so we can adapt these things to our practices.

When someone spring cleans, it literally means that they clear out any old and unused or damaged items during the spring months. In our discussion, we have come to understand that this clearing is essential for removing any negative energies.

Therefore, we should create a cleansing ritual for which we are removing any and all items from the home that are no longer needed, and we can do this in a number of ways. If the item is in good condition, we could clean and bless it before giving it to a donation center.

If the item is damaged and cannot be burned safely, we must clean it and then take it to a local landfill or have it collected. It must be removed from the home; it does not need to be kept in storage, nor should it be.

However, if it can be burned and you have a safe space to burn it, you absolutely should do so. This destroys and purifies, disconnecting it and its energies from you, your home, and your loved ones.

Fire is also a strong element as we have come to learn, so using this opportunity to dance, sing, and pray is going to help energize you spiritually.

The other common thing that society has brought to our consciousness is the habit of detoxing. This is drinking and eating healthily to flush out any and all toxic elements from the body.

This is something we can adopt, adding traditional spices in recipes to show thanks to Africa and drinking blessed water to flush our internal energy.

Creating the right internal and physical energies in our bodies and homes can improve our mental health.

Mental health is no joke, and feeling good in our minds is as important as any other part of our lives.

In truth, this is where the spirits who have less-than-kind intentions can affect us the most by causing us to doubt, feel depressed or angry, or feel tired and then be unable to sleep.

Nightmares and fears are also examples of functions of the mind. I keep a journal for anything to do with my mindset, so this may be a useful tool for you to make use of.

If you are regularly having issues with your mental health, you can always seek help in a number of ways. No one wants you to deal with it all alone.

CHAPTER VII

How to Per-form Prayers

Prayers for Hoodoo spirits are powerful things, so we need to think about how but also *where* we perform prayers.

In this chapter, I'll give you some steps to take and some guidance on how to pray. We'll get into the items you need, how to arrange these, and then we will dive into some prayers that you can use.

What we will be putting together is our Hoodoo altar. This will be the spiritual hub of our home. We can use this altar to pray and do any work we want to undertake.

What you will need: You'll need a quiet space. This is a sacred act and should be treated as such, so either choose a specific section of a room or a small room of its own, ideally a place where only you or family can attend, as you do not want negative influences in this space. You also need a flat surface and storage space. A floor will do for the flat surface, but as you will need to store anything you are using for spells or prayers, storage like a vanity table might be the best solution.

Additional items needed include a white cloth, two white candles (which can be any height or width), pictures or figures of the saints or spirits you are channeling, incense burner, holy water (Zamzam water or Florida water can work, but blessed water is best). Also, calming scents can help, but they are not essential.

You will also require flowers, salt, and any special stones you need, such as birthstones or stones for your chakra. For each of these, you need a small dish or bowl that has been cleaned in saltwater.

Lastly, soil is needed. The source of this soil can be related to your prayer. Much like burial, this can help with certain aspects of your life. You'll also need a bowl for this.

Once you have all these items, you'll need to arrange them as follows:

1. Place the white cloth on the flat surface. At the back of the surface, place one candle on the left-hand side and one candle on the right-hand side.

2. Between the candles, place the pictures (framed) or figures you are invoking. In front of that, you need to place the incense in the center of your space.

3. At the front of the altar, you will need to place several small dishes into which you add the salt, stone, and soil.

4. Once set up, you are ready to pray.

5. To pray, you address the spirits, light the incense, and sprinkle the table and all of the objects with the blessed water.

6. You can then lead by saying, "Dear spirit, my name is..." Here you introduce yourself, offering thanks and asking for what it is you need. For example, you can say, "Spirit, I need guidance on my love life," or whatever issue you need their guidance on.

Who to Pray To

There are a lot of spirits you can pray to. However, the stronger spirits are the Rada loa. For this example, we will talk about Legba, who is a spirit that is the guardian of the crossroads.

In old tales, it is said that blues musicians would sell their souls to the demon Legba, but Legba is not a demon; rather, this spirit is a trickster. It is a powerful spirit god who can influence reality and influence our path in life.

We can pray to Legba by drawing his symbol, which itself represents a crossroad, and chanting, dancing, singing, and holding a candle.

We use the vibration frequencies to channel the spirit and to ask them to visit us to allow our souls to enter the spirit realm.

We can chant things like "spirit, guard the door" or "spirit bless the house."

A typical chant may go like this:

"Family of the father,

Family of the mother,

We dance here,

We dance in this place.

Spirit guard the door."

For the line "we dance in this place," you can say what city you are in, or you can say in the home.

All the while, you'll need to be rhythmically moving, turning left then right on the spot, raising and lowering your candle.

If you don't have a prayer group, purchasing some audio of traditional rhythmic drumming will help. Again, vibrations of music can help us to communicate with the spirits.

Other Rada loa you can pray to include the following:

Ayizan, the first priestess, or mambo, who is a golden color and represents mysteries of initiation and the natural world.

Ayida-Weddo, who is the rainbow serpent and represented by white and green. This spirit takes offerings of white eggs, rice, and milk and represents fertility.

Loko, who we see as the patron healer represented by plants and trees. He is also the husband of Ayizan and is involved in initiation.

Then there is Danbala, who is one of the most important of the spirits. He is the great white serpent—the sky father. He moves between land, sea, and sky to create life. He too will be drawn to offerings of white eggs, but he can also accept coconut, rice, and certain perfumes.

Who to Worship

When we look at other cultures and religions, there is one definitive and right answer to the question, "Who should I worship?" And this is really the big difference and divide between Hoodoo, Voodoo, and other religions.

You see, while the spirits need to be acknowledged and accepted, they will need to be prayed to, and while you should make time for them in your life, Hoodoo practices are an evolution—a deviation from what Voodoo was.

So, in Voodoo, you worship the deity of your tribe or your ancestors. In Hoodoo, you acknowledge this deity and embrace them, but you worship God, or Yahweh if you choose to.

God from Christian churches is important to the Hoodoo belief, again due to that influence of the slave trade displacement. Hoodoo grew as a mix—a blend of cultures and ideas—where that idea of worship became that you could either worship God or the gods of Africa.

This is the biggest benefit of Hoodoo, especially if you believe in God. However, it is also the fact that there is more to creation and this world of ours than the Bible says.

It also isn't so strict that not believing in God gets you kicked out of the club. In fact, there are a great many Hoodoo sources who do not believe in God.

Ifa

There is a myriad of spirits that we can pray to, but we also pray to our ancestors. This is because it is said that they can see the past and possible futures. This power comes from a spirit chief named Ifa, the chief of destiny.

This spirit is said to influence our luck and fortune, and it allows the ancestors to see our fates. This, in turn, allows them to guide us and show us where we can begin to divine our best path.

This is the spirit you would pray to if you wanted to turn bad luck around or to ask for an omen to guide you.

Devil Worship

Witchcraft is often blamed on or associated with the devil, Lucifer. However, the truth is that this link was a weapon made by the church who used many means to undermine other faiths.

Even now, there are people who bring spiritualism from their faith in archangels, which is something that the church has tried to block.

Spiritual beliefs, however, are important to many of us who are trying to make sense of a world that has so many elements in play. This is why Hoodoo adjusts and combines—because that is what we are taught.

If the devil was at the heart of Hoodoo, there would be no healing spells and no spells for blessing others. And while there are less-than-pleasant tricks, the truth is practicing tricks can have consequences for the person casting the spells.

Hoodoo is about worshipping the earth, as well as the history that came before us and that we leave behind. The devil is part of the Christian faith, yes, and fearing the devil, and hell is important, as this reminds us of the consequences of meddling in magic with cruelty in our hearts.

However, there are those who do believe they can or have been able to conjure up the devil. While I personally discredit this idea, the attempts are all too real. That said, the simple fact will remain that summoning Lucifer is much more common in mainstream cultures.

Saints and Spirits

No one can fully change who you are, but you can adapt. One of the ways that our ancestors adapted our prayer to hide from slave masters was to find saints who aligned with spirits.

Danbala, for example, is represented by snakes, and St. Patrick has a relationship with snakes in the Bible, so our ancestors paired these. This is why saints like Peter, Patrick, George, and their ilk are kept on powerful coins or amulets that come into play during ceremonies.

But what about the spirits? There are many—far more than I could name. However, a couple are Sakpata, the spirit of the earth, and Xevioso, the spirit of justice and thunder. You will see spirits like Mawu and Lisa (sun and moon) represented in practices a lot and many saints paired with them.

Another example could be the patron saint of justice, Martin de Porres, who pairs with Xevioso. Praying to this saint would in the past, conceal the prayer to the spirit. Having a coin or medallion of Martin in a mojo bag for a justice spell amplifies that spell.

I mentioned Ifa earlier, and Ifa has a saint with whom to pair. Therefore, you can use Saint Boniface, the patron saint of good fate, to guide you.

Coin

Are you superstitious? This is a question I get asked a lot. I suppose in the eyes of someone looking at my life, the answer is yes. I have beads for protection, I pray for guidance, and I ask for forgiveness if I make mistakes.

I am constantly thinking about my actions and behaving in a way that I feel is kindest, even if that kindness is to say no. While this specifically might not seem superstitious, I believe that we are judged on how we act.

When I pray, I promise that I will make efforts to be kind and open to all those around me, even if they are ignorant. That kindness is my offering for the most part.

I have mentioned Legba a few times. He is the spirit of the crossroad and is a powerful entity who controls doorways to the world of spirits. So, to make him happy and to bring me luck, at night when I know it is not so busy, I head to a crossroad.

I cross the road, heading east, and halfway across, I stop and flip a coin, asking for luck or for a small blessing.

The coin I flip? Well, it is a coin showing the patron saint of luck, Cajetan. He represents the unemployed and gamblers and is the patron of Argentina.

When to Pray

Unlike many other cultures, there is no one right time to pray. You may pray every night or every morning, or you might make prayer time every Sunday. There is no rule on this front. There are days where prayer to spirits is stronger, and this is around All Saints' Day, the autumnal equinox.

This time is very important as it is the time at which the realms of the living and the spirit are the closest and thus when we are most likely to see spectres and feel connections.

This is reflected in many European cultures, where on All Saints' Day, the graveyards are adorned by hundreds of candles. This is to give thanks to the dead and their spirits.

Prayers in graveyards at this time are most likely to be heard, but again, the intent and intensity of the prayer is something to be careful of.

Asking for healing and blessings is fine, but asking for anything out of spite may invite the wrong energies into your life. But I would definitely suggest making a visit to a graveyard around this time of the year a tradition.

Particularly if you have a graveyard you can visit where your ancestors are laid to rest, paying respects to them is going to be deeply beneficial around this time.

I personally make a point of praying twice a day, in the morning to my ancestors and in the evening to the spirits, asking for guidance and then protection. But as I have said, prayer is a deeply personal part of our belief, so there is no one right way to go about it.

However, I will note that spirits will not assist those who expect help but do not pray. This may seem obvious, but I thought it worth noting all the same.

Meditation

The mind is a powerful thing, and in the modern world, it can be tough to find a balance. This is where meditation comes in. While I have and will continue to mention this subject in some form or another, I thought it best to delve into it a bit more here.

But first, you may be asking yourself, *What is meditation?* Mediation is the act of aligning the mind, body, and spirit. This is done by bringing each together in a calm, relaxed state, the intent of which is to help cleanse the energy of the self and move toward enlightenment.

Meditation has its roots in the Himalayas and the Tibetan monks that reside there. They believe that the body holds the soul, and upon death, it is released to join the spirit world.

Meditation is the disciplined pursuit of pure intent, both of heart and mind. As we are looking to work with the spirits and need our intent to be pure, meditation is therefore something we can adopt (although adopt is the wrong word as ancestral meditation is already a facet of Hoodoo and is something widely performed).

It is used in Hoodoo as a form of extended prayer, where the ancestors are consulted on decisions and omens. Below, we look at how you can carry out this meditation.

You will need: A quiet, isolated place, ideally where you are able to sit on a flat surface. You will also require candles, incense, a rug or mat to sit or kneel on, and a focal point for your prayer.

1. With candles lit on either side of the focal point, which could be your altar, lay your rug or mat before the item you are praying to, and light your incense.

2. Ideally, the incense should be a soft smell that you find calming, as harsh smells may distract your mind.

3. You can now kneel or sit cross-legged at the altar. Your prayer does not need to be complicated. Close your eyes, clear your mind, and whisper your prayer softly to the altar. An example of a simple prayer would be, "Spirit of the father, spirit of the mother, commune with me."

4. Some people will also use soft music, which is advisable, but again, do not use anything too energetic or disruptive. I'd also try to stick with CDs, tapes, or vinyl, as online streaming ads can be distracting. The key thing to remember is to keep your breaths slow and calm, with one deep inward breath through the nose and then one long slow breath through pursed lips. This slows your heart and calms your body, which, in turn, clears your mind.

5. Repeat the prayer several times, allowing your words to float.

6. Once you have finished your meditation, it is important to bless the area again and put away the rug and candles.

CHAPTER VIII

Hoodoo Dressing

When we prepare for a date or a night on the town, we may wear our lucky bracelet. While that concept is part of what we mean here, that isn't everything. When we say Hoodoo dressing, we aren't always referring to the clothes someone wears.

Hoodoo dressing is the preparation of a spell—the steps we take to make sure we are putting our best efforts into the spell. To show you examples of what you might do to prepare for a spell, I decided that it might be a good idea to talk about some of the things you'll come to know in the world of conjure.

We are going to look at a few traditional Hoodoo divination practices and how we might prepare to give a better idea of how we might set up this particular spell. Some of these things should be relatively easy to replicate, while others will take a bit of preparation to perform (though not much).

All of the items mentioned can be substituted; I cannot express enough how important that is. If you do not have an herb or spice, you can replace it with something to achieve the same effect. Seek advice from a local priest if you are unsure.

Here, we will look at steps we can take to prepare, the omens we must look out for, the consequences of ill intent, and how we begin to pay respects.

Divinations

Predicting the future is a form of magic that humanity is obsessed with. Predictions are made through astrology, numerology, or even by using computer programs to predict events. It sounds like science fiction or fantasy, but there is evidence of clairvoyance throughout human history.

While we use the term "divinations," this is a form of fortune-telling. There are a few methods to cover. First, there is what we will call cleromancy, which is rolling a collection of small items and reading the pattern they form.

These items can be dice, coins, sticks, or bones, for example. These items are always kept in a traditional cloth or leather sack, which is tied. This sack may have a braided string that is soaked in oils at its neck. The pieces are likely soaked in oil and spice to imbue them with the magic of the diviner.

Astrology and card-reading also have some African tweaks in Hoodoo, with scents and cards hand-drawn with African symbols and drawn whilst chanting.

This kind of divining is common in many cultures, but the variations in Hoodoo incorporate elements; the table on which the reads are performed will have traditional cloths, pots of water, and earth.

It is interesting to me that many African versions of these practices have detractors. (Yes, psychic mediums are commonplace.) This is partly because of a spiritualist movement that is happening in the world.

However, it is also informed by human curiosity, a thing that I hope leads to more traditional African practices being accepted in the same way.

Actions

The practice of Hoodoo and the actions we take also require a bit of preparation. I wanted to touch on some of those before we get into the kinds of preparations a practitioner may take.

Seeking is where we ask the spirits to help us attain something. This is usually salvation or forgiveness and is normally carried out at a church or in a congregation. Finding yourself a community is, therefore, a good idea. Social media makes this much easier than it might have been in the past.

This is especially true in places where Hoodoo communities may still be hidden away for fear of persecution.

We will also need to be prepared. Having your spices, oils, and items for Hoodoo conjure ready is important, but finding a spiritual supply point, such as an apothecary, will be incredibly important. You can also look for stores that supply other things, such as utensils and dishes.

Buying glass bottles, either from a store or online, is a good habit. You see, bottles are important. From wishes to dreams, many things can be written down and put in a bottle with an herb or root, or they can also be hung in trees or near/in the home to ward off unwanted spirits or witches.

Having blue glass bottles hung in front of a faint blue wall will trick a spirit into thinking the house cannot be passed, making it turn away.

Another action to take is to make sure that you have cleansed before bringing your first new items into the home. This protects them from any lingering negative energy.

Preparations

Much like stretching before a jog or eating breakfast before a busy day, preparation is key in Hoodoo. This preparation time will put your energy in the right place and help you ready your mind for the work.

When we have set up any spell or action, our prayers are an important part of what we need to do. We can ask for guidance from our ancestors, and for their protection, during the spell.

While the power of the spirits could be enough, we must understand that there are a few things we need to do to give our spells and prayers, the best chance to work. This includes burning oils, burning incense, using herbs, utilizing spices, using earthen colors, and praying over these items.

Lastly, I would suggest "smudging." This is the act of ceremoniously burning a bundle of sticks and paper wrapped with string and soaked in oil. Also, there are leaves or roots within the stick's paper to imbue the smoke with power.

We light the bundle in a large stone or ceramic bowl, allowing it to burn down to ash. Then, we envisage our negative energy, doubts, and fears raising with the smoke and dissipating into the sky.

This act can clear our minds and souls before we make any preparations. In clearing any of our own negative energy, we are not opening ourselves to misinterpretation of intent.

All materials should be cleaned with blessed water and used with a clear mind and clear soul. Anger or misplaced intentions could make the spell go wrong.

Once cleansed, any items we are using for a spell can be soaked in spices or oils that complement the spell itself.

Praying over these items, then setting a calm space for the ritual with complementing scents and candles to bring natural elements closer together, you can then lightly sprinkle dirt and water over the area you intend to use.

Clothes Make the Man

Now, I know I said that dressing didn't mean how you dress, and that is true. However, I also thought it would be a good idea to talk about clothes, both traditional and modern, and address some misconceptions.

First off, sashes, sarongs, and loose-fitting styles of clothes are traditional, yes, because they reflect the climate of Africa. However, these clothing choices are not essential; dressing comfortably is the only rule. Be who you are.

There may be a need to wear something looser for moving during ceremonial dances or prayer, but by no means are any clothes banned.

Wearing necklaces, pendants, or bracelets is preferable if they are comfortable for you, but they are not essential for every day. I would definitely advise wearing bracelets, as wearing ones with engraved beads showing symbols of the spirits can help you bring that energy with you wherever you need to go.

Clothes being an important part of your identity is a modern world concept. The truth is, being clothed at all is a blessing, and being thankful for this blessing is hugely important. It is always worth remembering how lucky we are in a developed society, where so many of our brethren struggle so much.

Having an open and compassionate heart is important and can lead to new levels of enlightenment.

Ill Omens

We see everything with our eyes, but that is not the same as understanding it. We may see a headline that a storm has rocked the next town or city over or that a flock of birds was found dead in a field, but we might not understand this message.

Omens are something that goes back centuries to our heritage. They are a fascinating phenomenon to research. Sudden crop death, a drastic drop in temperature, and even storms are examples of these omens.

Signs are out there for us to see. I have seen reports of livestock dying en masse after succumbing to diseases. While science claims that it was just a disease, you could look at that as an omen. This could be a warning that the land is cursed or that this is a trick being played.

Sudden weather or natural disasters are, as I say, omens. However, these are more so due to Mother Nature, and she is telling us that she is not happy.

We need to respect Mother Nature at all times. She is the one who nurtures us. When she sends us a message, we need to accept responsibility and pray for her forgiveness.

A number of times over the last decade in the United Kingdom, farmers complained of snow in spring months, which has hampered their ability to raise cattle and crops, and as such, they were concerned as to why this happened.

While the modern thought process would assert that this is simply a manifestation of global warming, the truth is most likely that Mother Nature is asking us to pay attention to what we are doing to the world.

Omens are not always negative, as we will discuss shortly, but the negative omens are the ones that make the most headlines. One of the most famous phenomena is hail. We have hundreds of instances of sudden, out-of-season hail. Again, this could be attributed to global warming, but what if there is a different meaning?

Good Omens

There is a good omen for every bad omen, and for every red sky in the morning, there is a red sky at night. We often hear some people say, "you make your own luck," which is to say that you have to put in the effort to make luck work for you.

And this is true of Hoodoo. We can spend a lifetime looking for omens and ignoring the opportunities around us. Seeing a good omen for what it is and acting on it is the only way we can ever truly capitalize on the positive.

Have you found something once considered lost or won on a scratch-off card? Give thanks to the spirits for the luck. Look for other opportunities, such as a new job or promotion; opportunities come in many forms.

We need to understand that we may be experiencing a swell of positive spiritual energy, and we need to follow it. Living in fear of consequences stifles our potential, but so does being blind to the energy around us.

Curses and Revenge

I have mentioned that magic, especially magic performed with ill intent, can bring consequences. While these consequences are not always obvious, it is worth noting that magic has come up in more than a few instances of tragedy.

In Honolulu in 1951, 85 men died, having had "excessively violent dreams." This was explained by a doctor as an acute sleep syndrome. However, it was widely believed that this was a "nightmare hex" created by a powerful priest.

While it is unclear if there was revenge against any suspect, in this case, there are examples of revenge being taken over spells. In fact, there is one that is quite famous.

On September 11th, 1997, a ferry called La Fierte Gonavienne sank near Haiti, and an estimated 200 people died from the catastrophe. US ships and divers were called in to help recovery efforts, and some strange things were noted about the sinking.

First, the boat sank just 50 yards from shore, having capsized just shy of returning. Survivors noted that the boat's internal doors could not be opened and that they had to leave many people trapped behind these doors. The boat itself was one of the few in the region to be metal rather than wood, and it had been on successful voyages.

Lastly, to retrieve bodies, the US coast guard divers had to cut holes in the vessel. The official explanation for the sinking was that too many passengers were on the same side of the boat, which caused the capsizing.

For the people of Haiti, however, there is another explanation: black magic. It was decided that a rival ferryman named Tio Djo must have cursed the boat out of jealousy. This led to angry Haitians burning the property and Ferry of Djo, an act of revenge for the loss of at least 200 lives.

This isn't the only instance of magic being at the center of an act of revenge. A great many witches were hung or burned at the stake because of their alleged acts. The Salem witch trials saw 25 witches executed, while hundreds of accused were killed during the European witch hunts.

Swallowed up by the Ocean

Beautiful, powerful, divine, and the giver of life, water is almost everywhere on this earth, and the few places it is not present are harsh and difficult to survive in.

It is for this reason that the sea and other bodies of water hold a great significance to the evolution of Voodoo and Hoodoo, Houdon, and other faiths. This is because it is still a common practice to pay an offering to the spirits lost at sea.

These ancestors are lost to the ocean, and as such, offerings of crops, fruit, medallions, and even valuable items are made to the ocean. This is to bring peace to those who were lost, but also to protect those making the journey, either to the new world or back home to Africa.

Millions of slaves were displaced in that time of our history, and many thousands, if not millions, were lost to the seas. They either died of disease or starvation on the boats or drowned in sunken vessels.

They were stolen to the new world but never arrived. They ever had their chance to earn freedom and carve out their new lives. The water came and claimed them; the harsh, cruel conditions on the boats claimed them.

So, we pay homage to them to help their spirits find peace and their way home.

CHAPTER IX

Hoodoo Empowerment

Our heritage is all around us. It is in the very fabric of our world, our daily lives, and not just our own, but the ancestry of those around us.

In New York City, there is a monument which was built where the burial grounds for African slaves who built the city lies. This moment is engraved with the symbols for the spirits and gods of the old world, of the tribal Voodoo and Hoodoo gods and spirits.

The heritage here is powerful, and I bring this up because it is a powerful place with a spiritual well at the center—a plateau where you can pray with the focus being on those slaves lost in that bygone era.

Power like this has had its fair share of misinformation, saying that ghosts are spiteful or that demons prey on people, that a home with spirits in it is cursed, and that danger is everywhere.

But this isn't the case. When a natural disaster happens, this is Mother Earth reclaiming control of her power, showing us that we must be grateful.

Which leads to how we can make deals and pacts with the spirits. When we are asking a spirit to cleanse our house, we can also say, "this is what I do in return".

We can ask, but greed can lead to spirits not wanting to help us. We can then offer our praise, worship, and energy.

We can embrace our culture and roots and the heritage we have long removed ourselves from.

Burning incense in doorways or using earthen colors is a good way of energizing and creating the feeling of spirituality in the home, and showing the spirits this respect is important.

Having pictures of our ancestors hung around or as part of our altars can show this respect for what came before.

Precious metals hold great power, so offering a spirit a coin or metal trinket in exchange for a blessing can help to build this relationship.

Possession Trance

When you hear the word "possession," you no doubt think of the Christian ideology of the devil or a demon taking over a body.

While it may be a scary thought, there is a good version of possession, and it is found in the Hoodoo and Voodoo cultures. A possession trance is where the person is held in the energy of a spirit.

This possession is one of energy, allowing the person to become more spiritual and to feel more like a spirit.

This is achieved in groups with chants and with oils and scents and candles, but it can take your mind to much deeper places.

When you do this, you'll see what I mean. It is not about the control of the person but about the elevation of that person to a new understanding.

This almost convulsive reaction to the energy is treated as a sign of its malevolence by many cultures, but to experience it firsthand is to know its divinity. Often, this sort of possession occurs at festivals or gatherings and is expressed by the spirit dancing through the possessed individual, who is left unharmed after the fact.

Many who have been asked about their experiences when they were possessed in this fashion were unable to remember it, though they were unharmed.

Powerful Places

Powerful places exist in our world, not just the obvious places you may be thinking of. Churches are obviously very powerful, but there are other places of power. Lakes, rivers, and forests are powerful places, for example.

Trees can be hundreds of years old and have absorbed a lot of energy. The roots of trees are literally part of Mother Earth, so they are a powerful thing. As we know, roots are part of many spells, and a tree's roots are especially potent.

In fact, I think it is no coincidence that the roots and branches of trees resemble veins. This is why we have begun to see wishing trees, places where people go and hang ribbons from the branches of trees to empower their wishes.

Trees near churches are growing on holy land—on blessed land—so using this location to meditate or to pray can be a good way to draw more energy into the prayer. Soft, rhythmic chanting can also allow for vibrations to pass from you into the tree and from the tree into you.

Lakes and rivers are powerful for entirely different reasons. Water has been a constant and continuous theme in our journey. Where the water empowers, the water purifies, and rivers and streams carry this power with them.

Water is used to baptize, to birth, to cleanse, and to purify. It carries life in it, and it washes away that which it does not need.

Many songs tell of rivers and their importance, and this is because Africa taught our ancestors that water is the most precious of all the elements, for it is from water and dirt that crops grow, and it is from crops that people and animals thrive.

Without the majesty of the element of water, nothing could thrive—nothing could survive—and that is a truly terrifying notion.

When we pray, lay tricks, or give blessings, we incorporate water where we need it, even if it is simply to put out the flames.

Performing any conjure near water can help to empower it by the simple act of being near such a wealth of natural energy.

Animal Offerings

We touched on blood and animal offerings earlier, but I wanted to talk about it and clear up any misconceptions. So, in Benin, Voodoo remains largely unchanged. It is much closer to ancient art than Hoodoo is now.

Here, animal offerings still occur, but not in the way you may imagine. Tribal dance, chanting, and plinths to the spirits are all in play. The spirit plinth is approached, and a man or woman offers a wooden steak, which they tap into the mound around the plinth.

This is a contract, as all magic is a contract—a promise that you will give something back to the spirit. For people who rely very heavily on crops or on livestock, these are seen as the most valuable offerings.

When the person who entered the pact is satisfied that the spirit has delivered on the prayer, they will take a goat (or pig or chicken) and cut its throat the same way they would for food. This is the first step in clearing the misconception. The animal is not tortured, nor does it suffer.

The fresher the blood, the more potent the thanks are, and the more satisfied the spirit will be. Any animals killed for these offerings are then used for food, so there is no waste, and their skin and feathers are used for materials.

Skulls, for example, can then be utilized in other spells. If someone is complaining of head pain or sickness, this can be transferred into the skull from the person's head through ritual and prayer.

This applies to many ailments, where a pain or sickness can be moved through this ritual of transfer into something else. This actually gives me the opportunity to talk about another misconception.

Voodoo Dolls

Voodoo dolls: we've seen them in films and read about them in books. The evil Voodoo priest presses a pin into the stomach of the doll, and the victim falls over in pain. Now, these dolls do exist, and there is a deep root for this kind of magic. However, this is in Wicca, not Hoodoo or Voodoo.

Yes, you read that right—Voodoo dolls aren't from the practice of Voodoo. They were labeled that way to go along with the narrative that Voodoo, Hoodoo, Vodun, and all of those beliefs should be considered evil.

Now there are human-shaped figures and dolls that hang around in many Hoodoo and Voodoo practices. These normally represent spirits or concepts like fertility or wealth, for which are being prayed.

That being said, in Wicca, European witches make use of these effigies, but not always in the way you might expect. In fact, that was one human effigy that became incredibly popular.

In 1998, during that year's soccer world cup in France, English soccer player David Beckham became the subject of national fury when he cost England a knockout game against Argentina. Beckham got sent off for kicking an Argentinian player.

England went on to lose the game, and soccer fans reacted by burning and even hanging effigies of the player.

Staying in England, Guy Fawkes attempted to blow up England's parliament in 1605. He was hanged, drawn, and quartered, but now, every November 5th, Guy Fawkes is commemorated on "bonfire night," where all across the United Kingdom, people burn effigies of "The Guy," commemorating his failure.

I believe this is why Beckham was met with this action. This action also goes to reinforce that Europeans have closer ties to effigy dolls than Voodoo does.

Locked In

If you go to Paris, Sydney, London, or many other cities around the world, you'll find bridges with hundreds of padlocks. These are either engraved or painted with people's initials. This act is an indication of love and an attempt to lock that love in forever.

Interestingly, these padlocks, and this idea of them bringing us love, is one found in modern Hoodoo, where the padlock is held with a candle and the hair of the one looking for love.

This hair, usually little more than a few strands, is pushed into the hole of the padlock, which is then shut locked and buried in the garden of the one seeking love. This makes a lot of sense, as slaves and tribal women may find suitors hard to come by.

Now, the bridges I have mentioned have been a subject of controversy, and the padlocks have begun to be removed in many cases, as this is seen to be causing damage to the bridges. The padlocks keep appearing, however, as the believed power of the act outweighs the perceived consequence.

Strange Ingredients

Many things can be offered to the spirits, but one that is somewhat common and easy to obtain is alcohol. This is often held in the mouth and finely sprayed onto a communal prayer monument.

However, a few drops during a standard prayer can help. This is to make the spirit "drunk," which may make the spirit less fearful of wards or protection spells.

Many alcoholic beverages are pre-spiced, but spices can be added if you feel that this is something that you need to incorporate in your spell-crafting.

Another thing to know is that there have been claims of Voodoo or Hoodoo poisoning, where the victim has been exposed to poison from strange places. Pufferfish, snake venom, and even plants that have toxic properties are all claimed to have been used in spells.

These ingredients are not only incredibly difficult to find but extremely dangerous to boot. For example, pufferfish venom can kill on contact, so handling such a fish is incredibly risky.

But poisons and alcohol are just part of the equation. The last and least surprising but most dangerous material to use is gunpowder.

Gunpowder is an ingredient some utilize, alongside poisons and alcohol. This is a disaster waiting to happen, but gunpowder is a blend of natural elements that are very powerful.

Dance

There are a great many African traditions, and many of them revolve around the dance and music of the nation.

While it is easy to explain dances, there is a massive divide between being able to explain a dance and explaining the power of that dance. Everyone can dance to some extent, but not all can dance with spirituality.

The intensity and emotion are much more apparent. This is because, in many dances, the spirit dances through the person. Even during festivals, there are traditional dancing garbs such as Zangbeto.

A Zangbeto looks like a hair or straw tent but is intricately designed. It is worn over the top of the dancer and adorned with colors and materials for the occasion and region. The design is large and airy to allow for much more control over rhythmic movements.

The only thing I can suggest to really grasp the energy, power, and depth of the importance of these dances is to witness them firsthand.

Spiritual Journey

When our home calls, we should consider going. Spiritual pilgrimages are not exclusive to any one culture. This idea of a prodigal son or daughter returning from a distant land to their ancestral home is done repeatedly in cinema and books.

This is because the idea of fitting in, belonging, and being complete are of the utmost importance to us all; just speak to anyone who has emigrated from one country to another, even one city to another.

The need to know or return home is one we have all felt at one stage or another. This is why the term "feels like home" resonates with us all.

Visiting Africa and seeing the roots of the magic and the culture is a journey that may be something your soul is already yearning for.

This would also help improve your connection to your ancestors, as it is a journey that shows a devotion to history. Many higher priests of Hoodoo and Voodoo make this journey to meet elders and seek otherwise unavailable items elsewhere.

While I know that a spiritual journey such as this may not be attainable for everyone, taking the time to research your roots is. Books and documentaries on the subjects of Africa, African culture, and the effects of the slave trade are readily available in our modern information age.

This means that not only is it possible to self-educate, but it is now easier to do so than at any point in our history.

CHAPTER X

How to Make Mojo Bags

In the movies, it goes something like this: A witch or priest takes out a small leather pouch and puts in a tooth, an eye, and some droplets of blood. The witch or priest shakes the bag furiously, screaming something unintelligible, and suddenly, the once-dead monster rises again.

While this depiction is another example of a Hollywood exaggeration, the truth is that the bag shown is either a mojo or hex bag.

Mojo bags are similar to but different from hex bags. Both are small but powerful spell items. Each uses similar materials and techniques and can even be prayed to in the same way.

However, where the two begin to vary is in the intent of the person making the bag or the contents of the bag itself.

While these normally follow a certain set of preparation basics, the more you personalize the bag, the more powerful it has the potential to be.

But what will you need? Well, this is a difficult question to fully address as the answer is almost anything (except, perhaps, eyes, although fish eyes could be useful).

You see, you can use coins, stones, dirt, roots, herbs, and even specially-carved items. Yes, you can use bone and animal parts too, but these will only be for specific spells. Also, it is very unlikely that you'll be creating a spell for instant use.

Many of the spells created in these bags are intended to work over a period of days and weeks, if not months.

So, let's start with something simple.

Let's say you want to make a mojo bag to empower your partner. You will start with a cloth that can be any color, but the traditional mojo bags are red. In that red piece of cloth, you will put a small citrine stone, which is a crystal for power.

Add to this a trinket that reminds you of your partner or that is important to him or her. If your companion is a guitarist, a guitar pick might be a good trinket to use. Add to this some dirt. In this instance, the dirt can come from various places to improve the effectiveness of the stone.

For example, if you add dirt from home, your partner will carry the protection of spirits with them wherever they bring the bag.

Then, you will fold and twist the bag to make it as small as possible. Then, tie it shut. Depending on the size of the bag, it can be carried as a trinket but should remain hidden.

Part of the idea of hiding it is because the magic is, and should be, deeply personal to the practitioner. However, this is also because displaced slaves adapted to keeping practices secret from their masters.

Hex Bags and Modern Witchcraft

Hex bags are a version of mojo bags popularized by TV and film, where the creator puts a powerful curse on a victim. While this isn't wholly true, hex and mojo bags can be used to bring bad luck or bad energy to another.

This is an energy that should not be messed around with, but it is possible to use. However, our mainstream understanding of hex bags stems more from European Witchcraft; they were left in bedrooms or houses to help cure the sick and largely to prevent death, not cause it.

Witch bottles are actually still common. In the UK in the 1980s, a small pill bottle was found on the banks of a river. This bottle, a witch bottle, contained a few teeth, urine, and coins.

The spell is specified to cure toothache. Although clearly designed to heal, this practice was illegal throughout North America and Europe during the slave trade era, thus forcing practitioners to hide their work.

This bottle can be substituted with a small glass vial and a larger brown plastic bottle, the kind that modern medicines tend to come in.

And yes, bones and urine are common ingredients in many spells and incantations in Hoodoo.

In fact, many cleansing spells and rituals call for the use of urine, either of the house owner or youngest child, to help cleanse the house.

While there is little to support this assertion, it is my belief that this practice was learned by slaves in transit, as many sailors were rumored to use urine to clean their clothes. Urine, of course, contains ammonia, which is commonly used in many modern cleaning solutions.

One of the interesting things I have seen during my years of trying to learn more about Witchcraft and Hoodoo is how many European magic influences there are. Things like witch bottles and the improvisation shown in the habits of many witches are reflected in Hoodoo.

This is obviously partly due to a shared persecution, but it is also likely to do with a spiritual connection both share to pagan gods—that is to say, ancient elemental gods.

Mojo Bag Improvisation

Not every ingredient or item is available everywhere. This availability is determined by cost, climate, and faith. Many places where one faith is more or less prevalent than others leads to items of that faith being less common. For example, finding items for Muslim faiths is easier in places where that religion is more common.

This leads me to one of the most common themes we have discussed: the fact that we can improvise when it comes to most anything we need to make, from our spells, potions, and even incense.

Because of this, I wanted to demonstrate a few ways we can make mojo bags using everyday items. These are items that we can either freely buy or that we likely already have around the house.

The first version of our mojo bag is one you could try today.

What you will need: a small piece of white cloth, string, root, herbs and spices, oils, loose change, and a mortar and pestle.

1. For this version, we start by placing the cloth in the bed of the target, under their sheet near their pillow. After a few days, retrieve the cloth. This now has energy from their dreams, as well as having been in proximity to the target.

2. We take the herbs, roots, and spices and crush these together. Now, we would pick the ones based on the properties we wish to conjure, but the idea is the same. Once the ingredients are crushed, empty the pile into the center of the cloth, and add a drop of complementing oil.

3. Now, in this example, I am going to suggest adding a coin by way of an offering to the spirits. You will then fold up and twist the cloth, tying it off with the string. This bag can then be buried in a household plant or garden if the target is the self. It can also be hung somewhere nearby or kept on the target.

4. As this particular one was made with dreams, hanging it from the base of the bed could be useful, especially if the spell is adjusted for healing.

Now, I know what you might be thinking; I said you could try this today, but you do not have a mortar and pestle. These items can also be substituted. Bowls are easy to come by, but what do you use to crush things?

When I first tried to improvise, I used the handle of a rolling pin, but an old pepper shaker or empty jar (depending on the size of the bowl) can also work.

Our second version requires the following: a small piece of white cloth, string, roots, herbs, spices, and oils, a piece of paper, a pair of dice, and, as before, a mortar and pestle (or improvised equivalent).

1. Here, we prepare in a slightly different way. First, bury the cloth for three days, then dig it up. This allows you to bring the power of dirt into the bag. On the piece of paper, write what you need. In this example, we ask for luck, so all your ingredients should be able to amplify luck.

2. Mix the ingredients, and put them in the cloth as before. This time, pray over the dice and then add those before tying off the bag.

3. This one should be kept in a pocket or bag. Luck is a powerful mojo, and losing the bag may lead to a hex or to someone stealing that luck, so keep it close and also hidden.

Gris-Gris

I referred to the differences between mojo bags and hex bags, as the latter has much more negative connotations, but there is another term I want to discuss. This term is gris-gris, a voodoo word for the bags themselves.

The main difference here is that gris-gris bags require a blend of oils and herbs, whereas as with mojo bags, we can use both, either, or neither as we see fit. But in truth, you can refer to the bags you make as gris-gris, and most will know what you mean.

This transformation of terms or evolution of meanings comes from the displacement we speak of so often—millions of slaves from thousands of tribes came together. This was almost a human gumbo, which means there are many ways of saying the same things.

Interestingly, there are a few ideas where certain individuals' preferences influence the practices and the terms they use. However, the truth is that there is no right way of saying any one thing. The displacement of millions of people created this cross-influence of terms and ideas, languages, and spirits.

For example, gris-gris and hex bags work as a term instead of mojo bags in much the same way some people say computer games instead of video games or film instead of cinema.

The key is the parts of tradition and individuals you have been exposed to.

Traditional Dolls

Whilst Voodoo dolls are a misconception born from horror movies, there are several dolls made as traditional toys for young children, or for adults, to bring about specific blessings. These are made from twine, beads, and wood that are put together in such a way as to represent a person.

Ndebele dolls are traditionally for young girls, made by and gifted from their mothers, with the beads and twine replicating traditional dress. Xhosa dolls are for women and are worn around the neck on a length of twine.

This doll is a symbol that the wearer is ready to have children and is also blessed to be more fertile.

Another fertility doll, but carved from wood and painted rather than made, is the Akuaba doll. These are carried on the back, not front, of a woman looking to become pregnant.

Lastly, we'll look at hut dolls, these are also carved from wood and for the want of bringing a child, but they live on the top of a hut of an infertile or childless woman. This doll is then burned with the placenta when the child is born.

Shrunken Heads

Many items are referenced in popular media that don't exist, such as the Voodoo dolls we had discussed previously.

That said, there are equally as many items that don't seem like they could be real that definitely are which have deep cultural roots. This is the nature of misinformation and human understanding of our shared heritage.

What might surprise you is that shrunken heads are a real thing. If you were to travel to Oxford in the United Kingdom, there is a museum called Pitt Rivers. This museum is home to hundreds of African tribal items.

Everything from masks, shields, spears, and even items used for music can be found amongst the collection, but interestingly, before September of 2020, so could shrunken heads.

The heads were removed as they continued to spread misconceptions. One such misconception is that these originated from Hoodoo magic. The truth is these tended to be made from monkey skulls or sloth skulls, although some were from deformed human skulls.

These were not made as a punishment but were offerings to spirits. However, they do not come from Hoodoo. These, in fact, have their history in South America, another continent that would somewhat influence modern Hoodoo.

I had the opportunity to see this collection before it was removed and found these items fascinating. That said, I do agree that these simply made more correlations to the idea that African heritage is savage, and these items invoked more racist ideals.

Superstitious

You may be reading this and thinking to yourself that some of the practices in Hoodoo sound like superstitious nonsense, but what if I told you that there are already magic things we do every day?

One thing I really wanted to talk about is the idea of superstitions. These are the things we either do or avoid doing because heritage teaches us that this is the right way to behave. These small things act as a way of protecting ourselves from bad luck or curses.

Walking under ladders is bad luck, breaking mirrors is bad luck, and crossing the path of a black cat is bad luck. We sign the cross when we see a hearse, and husbands carry their partners over the thresholds of their homes.

The number 13 is unlucky. People wear lucky socks, lucky pants, and lucky charms on their jewelry. All of these things and many more are superstitions that have been normalized, despite the fact that many of them are about influencing energy and even luck, a core part of the Hoodoo faith.

One of my favorite things to point out to people who suggest that spirits are not real is this: Have you ever spilled salt? If you have, there is a chance that you have been told to toss some over your shoulder to ward off bad luck, in this case a spirit, and salt the ingredient of a protection spell.

There are thousands of small things like this that we do on a daily basis that we attribute to the protection of the self or the home in the name of luck. Yet, when you tell someone, you have put together a small pouch of trinkets for luck, this is treated as some strange alien concept.

Four Thieves

One of my favorite items to discuss that is very much a proven medicine is a powerful blend of wines, ciders, herbs, and spices called "four thieves vinegar." This vinegar, often made with garlic as the key ingredient, evolved during the spice trades and was said to cure the plagues of the era.

It typifies the evolution of our culture and beliefs and is solely drawn from natural ingredients. The mixture is stored for several days and is prayed over throughout.

It is just a fascinating thing that came to be a common cure for the plagues and illnesses of the time. Yet, when it was first introduced, it was likely met with the same skepticism many other magic and potions are met with.

CHAPTER XI

How to Perform Spells

Here we are in the end stretch of our beginner journey, and I really hope you've begun to understand the power and benefit of what we are doing together. I really feel that while what we have covered doesn't even begin to scratch the surface of all of the potential of Hoodoo, I do feel this will help you with the next questions to ask.

As such, I wanted to cover some more advanced things you can try or learn about to strengthen your connection to the spirit realm. Some of these spells and ideas are also put here to open your mind a little more, as you'll need to fully embrace the spirits to thrive.

For each of these sections to come, I'll guide you through what the technique requires, what items to use, and how the practice is currently used. The question is then yours to ask regarding what potential uses there are for these practices.

But be warned that many spells can have interesting side effects in ways that you may not have been expecting, from rashes and headaches to a cold or even bad luck. Making use of spirits is potentially dangerous.

Dream Smoke

One of the greatest mysteries of life, and one of the most complex parts of our existence are dreams. They have been written about, studied, and evaluated for centuries. They are deep and meaningful, yet they remain perplexing and mysterious.

Dreams are powerful, and our minds are more receptive than we know. Many have dreamt of messages from spirits and others. Songs, books, prophecies, and political movements have all been inspired by the dream state.

Communication through dreams is a very simple spell to attempt but a tricky one to master. All you need for this spell is mugwort, tobacco leaves, and lavender.

As you'll need a space to start a small fire, this is probably best done outside. Let the flames settle down to a light fire as you would a barbeque. You then burn the herbs down, calling out the name of the person you want to send the spell to.

Now some say to do this three times, some five, and some once. I say you should try this to see what works for you, but I have found three times is best. Once you have said their name, whisper your message into the smoke.

You'll want to do this spell at night or when the target is most likely to be asleep. You may receive a response in your dreams. This is also a good way to ask spirits to visit you in the dream world.

Instead of shouting the name of the spirit who you want to hear you, shout the name of a spirit or ancestor you wish to see. Then whisper that you invite them into your dreams.

Storm Protection

Storms and natural disasters are Mother Nature's way of showing us her truest power, and as such, we need to be mindful of protecting ourselves and loved ones during these times.

While prayer can go a long way in helping with protection from disaster, there are other steps we can and should be taking.

What you'll need: Comfrey root or angelica, white cotton, paper, pencil, and a thread of hair or nail clippings.

1. First, you'll need to take the pencil and write the name of the person you want to protect and the dates on which you need them protected. You then wrap the root and the hair or clippings in the paper and tie it with the cotton thread.

2. Now, this is where Hoodoo benefits from the Christian belief. You can read Psalm 22 over the root while you wrap it, or you can pray to the spirits for their protection.

3. When you tie this off, leave some excess string. Now there are three choices for you: You can tie it on the door of that person's home, have the person wear it as a necklace, or you can bury it in their garden. If they do not have a garden, you can bury it in a potted plant within their house.

This spell is a common and popularly-quoted one, as it shows all of the various parts of the good sides of magic. It also shows a healthy dose of respect for Mother Nature and her power, which is the power of landslides, earthquakes, tidal waves, and many other things.

Sickness

We have covered a great many ways of combating sickness in this guide, from mojo bags to milk baths, so we already have a few great things to try—but one more cannot be a bad idea.

What you'll need: several quartz stones, mortar and pestle, lavender, sandalwood, juniper, rosemary, a small piece of cloth, string, and incense.

1. Crush the lavender, sandalwood, juniper, and rosemary into a crushed blend, and set to dry. Once dried out, place the heap into a small piece of cloth with one small quartz stone, and wrap and tie it with string. Both the cloth and string can be soaked in lavender oil, but this is not essential.

2. Then, place quartz stones on a flat floor in eight compass points: north, east, south, and west, as well as northeast, northwest, southeast, and southwest. Now, if the sick person is able to stand, have them stand in the center holding the bag.

3. Both you and the sick person should then pray to the spirits for health and recovery. If the person is bedridden, you can place the stones under the bed in these positions. If you are unsure of your north and south position, buying a compass is a good idea.

Bad Omens

When you are performing spells, things can go wrong, and you'll begin to see signs that the spell has not worked as intended.

Black smoke is the first indicator that a spell has begun to go bad. If the smoke quickly disappears, then the spell was simply being resisted, but if the smoke is thick and continuous, then it is time to stop, cleanse, and consult a priest for advice.

When using tall candles, the candle breaking for no reason may mean that the spell will conjure unwanted or unexpected outcomes, and you should stop immediately.

With short candles or tealight candles, if the flame won't catch or the wick goes out quickly, you may not have enough energy to perform the spell. This could indicate the wrong ingredients, too few resources, or that the prayer wasn't made with conviction. If you persist and this still fails, you may need to check for protection on the target or hexes on yourself.

There are several little signs, things like misplacing keys or items for conjure, where someone may have put a hex on you. If you find yourself having a run of bad luck, it is time to cleanse the house.

In the wider world, omens of crop death and cattle death are key things to be wary of. This may be an influx of negative energies, so practicing magic around these times may lead to unexpected consequences.

Disposing of Old Materials

When we make a spell or put together a mojo bag, we have a few choices in relation to excess materials. Many items can be reused, and we'll talk about how to clean and reuse items separately, but disposal is important.

First, if it is something you cannot reuse, and cannot dispose of in the other methods we'll cover, then we need to start by praying over it, asking the spirits to remove any magic left in the items. This can then be thrown out in the garbage as normal.

Anything that can be buried does not need to have the magic removed. However, only bury this in your garden if it was used for blessings. If you wish to bury something and remove the magic from it, by all means, do so.

Anything that will be safe to bury can also be burned or cast into a body of water or stream. However, anything used for either a hex or a spell that has gone wrong should be prayed over for the magic to be removed, and then burned or washed down a stream.

Reusing of Old Materials

If an item can be reused, we first need to pray over it, asking the spirits to remove the excess magic in the item. Then, we need to clean the item.

Here, we use blessed, or Florida, water to clean the item. Once the item is clean, we should pray over it again.

It is also advisable to have two sets of items so you can have some clean and some in use at any time.

I would advise against trying to use any excess materials that have not been treated. So, for example, if you buy some tobacco leaves, and you take five out of the pack and use three when you come to a new spell, do not use the extra two; your previous intent is in those leaves until you clean them, so dispose of them with fire, burial, or in a stream.

As I noted, though, some items can be cleaned. Florida water can be used for leaves and other solid items, as these are easy to clear. As for spices or oils, any spillages should be cleaned and removed from use.

Suffering

One thing that many practitioners don't tell you is that spirits are more likely to listen to the prayers of the suffering. This is due to their benevolent nature. Returning to Marie Laveau for a moment, she teaches us this.

It is said that during her prayer sessions, she would pray in silence with hot peppers held in her mouth, bringing her intense pain. This was done to amplify her suffering so that the spirits might take pity on her.

I can't advise you to do this as spicy peppers can damage the skin in your mouth, so this is a really painful process. But it does raise some interesting questions as to when we should be praying and asking for help. Asking when we are not in need or are not honest about our needs may lead to the spell's failure.

This coincides with the idea of sins—notably greed. Greed is the action of always asking for more, even if more is not genuinely required or earned.

Familiar Practices

There is always a fine line between the truth and a lie. This line is often a mirror, where the opposite is true. That isn't always the case, and it can be that the truth has become blurred or twisted and that this new lie often contains a sliver of the truth itself.

This is especially true when the knowledge someone has of a time or of a series of events comes from Hollywood.

Hollywood has pushed a fair amount of lies onto society over the years. But there are also some misconceptions about magic, and Voodoo/Hoodoo in particular, that have some semblance of the original truth buried within.

The most prevalent one is salt. Salt is shown time and again to have intense magical properties in film, TV, and books. This is because it is a revered material, important not just in cooking but in spells also.

In folklore, salt is said to ward off bad ghosts, and this is part of its properties in our practices. The idea of creating a salt circle to keep ghosts or spirits out is one that may have its roots in a blend of Voodoo and Wicca.

In Hoodoo and Voodoo, materials, including salt, are sprinkled around the shrine of prayer, which allows the person who is praying to a spirit to block out unwanted entities.

This is not the only instance of an element of truth being reflected in Hollywood. Another pretty common one is where a spirit is shown escaping from an inanimate object. This is because many priests will try to bind or trap a spirit and then have that spirit do their magic work for them.

This belief has ancient roots and is seen in the belief of
jinn, or genies, powerful wish-granting spirits trapped
and bound to an inanimate object (in this case, a lamp). It
is believed that silver and iron have power over spirits in
fiction and have the best chance of binding a spirit.

CHAPTER XII

Frequently Asked Questions

We have almost come to the end of our journey, but there is still so much to learn—so many things to discuss. I wish that we could cover everything there is to know of the subject, but in truth, this book would be endless.

So, in this section, I want to address some things that didn't really fall into other parts of the book. I want to ask questions that get asked of me all the time, and I also wanted to take a look at some common questions about Hoodoo from the internet. I felt this was important to include as it may allow us to recap and to have just a little fun with Hoodoo.

This will also give me the flexibility to answer these questions in an in-depth way (or as in-depth as possible) while providing examples that you can go and take a look at.

It will also allow you to consider the next steps you can take in your journey of enlightenment. So, without further ado, let's have a look at those burning questions.

Can white people practice Hoodoo?

This question is one I get asked all the time, and it isn't an ignorant one. Many people are very clued up on what happened with their ancestry and wonder if this would affect modern people. The truth is, anyone can practice Hoodoo. Faith is a deeply personal thing.

People don't all believe in God, and people don't all believe in Allah. Hundreds of years ago, there were people who believed in Thor and Loki as gods. Faith is ever-changing and is located in the soul.

In fact, there are white people who practice Hoodoo as it is a faith of adapting and accepting that we are all the same at the spirit level.

If you feel like it speaks to your soul, who has the right to tell you that you cannot believe it? That's right, no one.

As I said, I can understand where this concern comes from, but the truth of the matter is that no race is defined by the actions of their ancestors; they can only build on these actions and repay the faith.

Does being Christian/Muslim prevent me from practicing Hoodoo?

Not in the slightest. People convert to other religions all the time, and looking for your roots in Africa is totally normal. All life came from Africa, so we all share a heritage.

Earth is our mother. Believing in Allah or God and also believing in Hoodoo spirits is fine. While most who regularly practice believe in God, the majority of work is done with spirits and, as such, the principal deity is not the only concern.

Where can I find an apothecary?

Unfortunately, apothecaries are not quite as common as once was the case, but they do still exist.

However, what is good is that many herbs and spices can be found in most supermarkets these days. Most good homeware stores will store the other items you'll need.

However, yes, you'll likely need to find a supply of some very special items. Improvisation is encouraged, though, and it is how our ancestors thrived. Black salt, for example, is salt mixed with charcoal or other black items.

For uncommon items, you may have to order off of the internet or look into what it is and find substitutions. For example, some roots have similar properties, so a replacement is always around.

For any offerings, a boiled white egg would work just as well as an offering of rice. Thus, it is often worth having a good look around your local stores to see what items you can make use of and how best to capitalize on their availability.

What if I can't find something?

Oftentimes, I am asked what to use if you can't find black salt or bone, and as I just said in the previous answer, improvisation and research really are key. Chicken bones make for easily accessible materials for small conjure or hexes.

One of the most common questions is, "What if I can't find a piece of cloth?" When we say a piece of cloth, it can be cut off of an old dishcloth or underwear, bedsheets, curtains, or even socks. Finding a replacement does not need to be difficult, nor does it need to cause you concern. Simply have a look around your house.

You'll find cloth in the home, rice in most stores, and stones in the garden or local park. And when you cannot, I always would just consider what can be used in its place.

One of my favorite tips is to look in thrift stores. You'll find all kinds of small dishes, fabrics, and containers in these places. One thing I like to grab from thrift stores is old copies of the Bible.

These tend to be worn and older, but this means they have soaked in a lot of energy from their previous owners. A cleanse or prayer should be used to remove negative energy, and the items should be good to go.

Can I buy this from Etsy or eBay?

Etsy is a really cool site, don't get me wrong. However, my only advice for purchasing anything online is to check the reviews first.

As with anything, if the reviews for a long-established store are bad, it is probably a good idea to avoid it. After all, you never really know someone online.

Etsy is full of great tips, guides, hexes, spells, and even handmade pendants and starter kits, but these items can be created at home with just a little work.

eBay is a tricky one, as there is a prevalence of fake or bootleg items on the site. Thus, I'd be extra skeptical about anything bought from there.

Can Hoodoo be practiced on a non-believer?

So, I have always assumed that this refers to hexes, so I would say perhaps don't hex anyone. But to answer the question, disbelieving in something does not protect you from it, although there are those who claim it does. However, would not believing in gravity make you float?

We are all exposed to hundreds of people every day to varying degrees, and each of those people has different beliefs, energy, or prayers or, as is the case sometimes, none of these.

However, if the people are not believers, it does not mean that the divine does not protect them. The truth is, good people may not believe, and that is okay.

What is a divination Jack?

A divination Jack is a small, egg-shaped charm used in divination to channel the energy of the person performing the spell. This, in some respects, is similar to a lucky rabbit's foot, as it works to channel the energy it is associated with.

You don't need one per se, as divination works differently for all of those with the gifts to do this, but having a talisman of sorts is always worthwhile. This can be one you have crafted or something you have found.

I'd personally always use something that has been blessed by a fellow practitioner of the magic, but this is purely my personal feeling and doesn't mean I am right.

Is the Lord's prayer suitable for cleansing work?

Of course, it is. I think most prayers are, to be totally honest. If you use a few various prayers, depending on the work you are doing, and this is the one that feels right for cleansing, then by all means, do so.

I think that it would be dishonest to suggest that there could be a prayer that doesn't work, as some prefer to show faith without prayer or through silent meditation.

One of the core things to always remember is that faith and the energy we draw from it are deeply personal, so finding where you are able to draw this energy from is key.

Are some people more accepting of supernatural events than others?

This is a question I get asked a few times a year, where people are really asking two questions at once. The first is this: Where does skepticism come from?

The idea of skepticism is something we as humans grow to have. It is challenging the normal, accepted way, and we are trained to push against those ideas of difference and change.

This is why cultures are all but wiped out when they are conquered. Hundreds of years ago, Odin was a god wor-shipped in Norse culture, but now he is a myth-—a story. This transition is seen time and again in our history, with Egyptian gods now consigned to memory and opinion.

This is because, to quote quite a famous line, history is written by the victors. The truth is seldom as clear-cut as the history-writers would have us think. This misinfor-mation is part of why skepticism exists—because we are taught one-half of the truth all our lives, so seeing another side of it feels alien.

The other part of the question that I think people are try-ing to grapple with is this: Is there an aptitude for magic?

In our stories and folklore, there are people who can and people who cannot perform magic, and I think this idea is one that informs this question. You see, whenever there is someone in a position of power, they have a tendency to say that others cannot do what they do.

This is where this belief that we cannot do something often comes from. However, Hoodoo shows us that no amount of oppression can stop our power and faith. This is the lesson of our ancestors—that no matter what happens, the spirits and God Himself are with you.

There are more experienced practitioners, but this is true of anything. For example, someone may be more experienced at using a computer. This doesn't mean that you yourself cannot learn to use that computer. The same is true with magic and Hoodoo.

Practice makes perfect, as the saying goes.

Do I need to paint my candle?

Candles come in a great many shapes, sizes, and colors, and people will often ask if there is any need or benefit to painting a candle. Now, there are a variety of answers to discuss here. In fact, you could have a rather long conversation on candle etiquette.

First, for general prayer, no, you do not need to paint a candle. There will, of course, be benefits to scented candles, especially when complementing meditation. However, for the most basic and general prayer tasks, a plain candle is fine.

And no, the candle does not have to be white. Colored candles work just as well, so if you want colors as part of your altar, you can coordinate. I personally prefer white candles, but again, this is one of those things that is profoundly personal to the individual.

Secondly, there are benefits to incorporating sigils and painting them onto the candle for cleansing, which could be a good way of doing this. If, for example, you do not have carved beads to hold this symbol on, you can use paint.

Then, of course, there is spell work, where the use of painted candles is a much more common practice. Symbols are often painted onto candles to amplify spells, both blessings, and hexes. This is especially true when the individual is asking for a specific spirit.

This kind of practice is still somewhat common, as cursing a rival is something many farmers and fishermen have been accused of, as we can see. Many candles are painted black for hexes, with the paint used mixed with herbs and materials to empower the spell.

I would advise against this kind of practice, as would many others, as you may be welcoming bad spirits and energy into your home and body.

Why hasn't my spell worked?

Many factors influence the potency of a spell, from the connection between the conjurer and the spirits to the items used. Such is the case that almost daily, you'll find a spell has failed someone.

It could be that something on the conjurer is blocking the spell or that the items they are using have been tainted. If placing a blessing or hex on another person, it may be that they are protected and that they cannot be touched by magic at that time.

The spirits themselves could be preventing you from the casting of the spell, in which case you need to begin to ask yourself why this is the case. You must then consider communing with the spirits as your next best step.

Another issue could be caused in the self. When we do not believe we can do something, we will often fail. This applies to many aspects of life, and as such, you need to keep a clear and positive mindset.

The other thing that could be causing the problem is your intent. You may be asking for something you either don't need or don't really want. The spirits will know what our intent is, and if the spell is coming from a dishonest place, the spirits may simply deny you.

Whatever the cause, if a spell fails, you need to consider what you can do to improve your chances next time you decide to do the work. You can then clear away any bitterness toward the spirits from your heart.

Can you buy a spirit?

This is one that came up as I was at a convention, and I was only asked it once, but as I was not able to answer at the time, I felt it right to answer here.

I had to do very little research, but I was able to confirm that you can, indeed, buy spirits. This is largely an act of desperation, but it is possible. The spirit needs to be bound to an item, which you then buy, but this does not come at a cheap practice.

That being said, I personally would advise against such an act as it is likely to bring the dissatisfaction of spirits to you. This is one of those questions which, even with my experience and knowledge, surprised me. This is why I tell you not to assume anyone knows everything.

Does non-African music work?

This question is usually asked in relation to dances, chanting, and/or prayer and meditation, so we will look at those three elements in turn and discuss the various considerations. The answer is a little more complex than a simple yes or no answer.

First, let's consider tribal dancing, and the first answer is a solid yes. However, there is a caveat; I would use more tribal-sounding music. More standard genres of music, especially when there are lyrics, tend to be much more simplified rhythmically, and the lyrics can be distracting.

Instrumental music with a complex tribal inspiration is good to use for tribal dancing in lieu of traditional music.

The second consideration is chanting or prayer, and for both of these, I would say that no, non-traditional music is not going to suffice. I know that there are those who may not agree with me, but singing and prayer are both deeply personal experiences, so removing the self from this is going to devalue it.

As for prayer specifically, hymns and prayer songs are always going to be preferred over chart music.

Lastly, for meditation, yes, other music works. However, I would advise against music that is too loud and energetic, as this can be distracting and can lead to pulling you out of the feeling you are trying to experience. Although I am sure you already know this, there are those who listen to whale songs or the sounds of the forest while meditating.

This is all about what relaxes you, so everything is fair game.

How do I know if a hex/trick is laid on me, and how do I counter it?

This question is not quite as complex as it seems, but again, I will break this down into its parts. First, we'll look into signs that you may be under the power of a spell, then we will look into how to remove it.

Mostly, you'll notice that something is definitely wrong, where you seem to be having bad luck all the time, aches and pains, or you are feeling tired and stressed, and there is no reason for this. Even feeling a cold breeze where you should not be feeling one could be an indicator.

The first thing to do is cleanse the self-using the methods we have discussed previously in this guide. Then, pray to the spirits to ask them to remove any magic of bad intent from you.

Once you have done this, look to see if the pattern continues. If not, then you can move on to laying tricks for protection. If the signs of bad luck continue, it is time to cleanse the house.

Once the house is cleansed, it will either be time to cast protection magic for the home; if the bad luck continues, it is time to consult a more experienced Hoodoo practitioner.

Can magic affect sports?

This is a question that comes up a lot because either a team is losing a lot or has a sudden upturn in fortune. There are countless indications of magic influencing sporting events, from the lucky numbers of players to pre-match rituals.

Croatian tennis player Goran Ivanisevic was granted the wildcard for entry into the 2001 Wimbledon tennis tournament, which he won, stating that his ritual included watching a children's TV program for luck.

An interesting curse from the worlds of both sport and video gaming has occurred, at least according to fans. The video game in question is the Madden NFL series, where the cover star is a player who has done well in the previous season.

When a new game comes out, the player has either a bad season or a season riddled with injuries. This interesting curse appears in other media, but none are quite as famous as this one.

So yes, I think magic can affect sports, and there have been accusations of curses on teams in the past. However, I imagine this will never be something we can fully prove.

Can I cast a spell on a meal?

There are times where the perfect example is hard to come by, but "saying grace" is literally giving thanks for the meal. Whilst this isn't exactly what is being asked, the answer is affirmative.

Meals can be blessed by asking for blessings, and spices and herbs that empower the dish can be added. I have referenced gumbo in our journey a bit, and this is because there is a reverence to this dish and its evolution.

Blessing a meal is something most people do without ever considering the fact that this shows an acceptance of the supernatural and spirits specifically. Meals are important, not just because they nourish us, but because they are delivered to us by our knowledge of the earth—a knowledge that is millennia-old.

Are you ever too old to start?

I think this is the perfect final question. As you have undoubtedly noticed, I like to reference sayings. There's one I have always wondered about: "You can't teach an old dog new tricks."

Is this true, and is this something that is applied to people as well? The answer is no. Many famous people had "late starts" to their successful careers, and many athletes flourished later in life. Not all success is attained early.

The fact of the saying is that it is easier to learn a new thing when young as the mind is more responsive and absorbs information easier. But this does not mean that it cannot be done—just that it is more challenging.

This is the same kind of conversation as the dreaded question, "What do you want to do when you grow up?" The truth is many people don't know, and some never find their calling. You may finish this journey and decide Hoodoo isn't for you.

Life isn't set in stone, and no choice is final. We must find what works for us and what makes us happy and foster it to the point we need for nothing else.

Finding that thing, regardless of what it is, won't be on a timer. It may get harder later in life, but that doesn't make it impossible.

Next Steps

We have come a long way, covering what Hoodoo is and what it is not. We discussed the misconceptions around black magic, devil worship, and Voodoo dolls.

We looked at traditional trinkets, dance, and materials. We delved into prayer, meditation, and what we can do to empower ourselves spiritually. We went over mojo bags and spells and cleansing our homes and selves.

And now we are able to answer our first question: "What is Hoodoo?" We can respond by saying it is a complex spiritual religion with many practices rooted in magic and prayer.

But we have one last question left to ask—one last thing to consider: What next?

What are the next steps of our journey, what should we do, and what can we do to deepen our knowledge and expand our horizons?

The truth is there are so many answers I cannot possibly provide them all, but there are a few I would quite like to share with you.

Firstly, I would say to learn. Go off into the world, grab some books, watch some documentaries, and learn. Absorbing the information of the culture is something that can only help to enrich your experiences.

There is a wealth of information out there, almost to the point of information overload, but looking for the information you need, that is a good place to start.

Secondly, I would take the time to find yourself. You've likely just scratched the surface of your own journey of self-discovery. Travel will help—seeing parts of the world that you have maybe lost a connection to.

While there are no specific places you should travel to as where you are drawn to is going to be very specific, do a little research into your ancestors. Where did they come from? Is it safe to travel there?

Thirdly, as I have touched on before, I would begin to look for social groups of like-minded people. As a writer, I am drawn to open mic nights and poetry slams. As a practitioner of Hoodoo, I am drawn to churches and religious gatherings.

Finding people who are like you and who have more or maybe even less experience in Hoodoo and spirituality is going to help you. Friendships built from shared experiences are good for the soul and mind.

This is honestly among the most important things we can do as individuals; humans are social animals, after all.

Lastly, I would always advise that whatever you do, love yourself. Make time to rest, relax, and recharge. The world we live in is so fast and frantic that we often forget to put care into the self, which is a real shame.

Finding a routine built around the concepts of self-care, be it exercise or home-cooking is important. These things bring positive energies to our homes and to our hearts, and we must embrace this.

This self-love leads to hope, which is a powerful emotion that we all need; it is the very feeling that we can do better and be better.

Loving the self, but not at the expense of others, is the Hoodoo and spiritual way. It is who we are and who we should always aim to be.